More Praise for
Coaching Your Kids in the Game of Life

"Ricky Byrdsong's approach of coaching as a parent gives fresh insight and new principles for parenting. It is a practical book with penetrating spiritual anchors."
Dr. Willie Richardson
Senior Pastor, Christian Stronghold Baptist Church—Philadelphia

"This book should be added to every home library and included on the shelves of school libraries across the nation. It should be considered required reading for parents of teenagers as well as those responsible for the education of our young people."
Dr. Randy White
Pastor, Without Walls International Church—Tampa
Author, *Without Walls: God's Blueprint for the 21st Century*

"This book meets one on the most critical needs of the hour . . . sane, solid, practical guidance for parents. The parental arsenal has a great new weapon to battle the barrage of 'politically correct' stupidity currently threatening the health of every family."
Charles Lyons
Pastor, Armitage Baptist Church—Chicago

"This book is a wonderful guide for parents, in order that we might fulfill the biblical exhortation to raise our children in the training and admonition of the Lord (Ephesians 6:4)."
Bishop Eddie L. Long, D.D., L.H.D.
New Birth Missionary Baptist Church—Decatur, Georgia

COACHING YOUR KIDS
in the Game of Life

COACHING YOUR KIDS
in the Game of Life

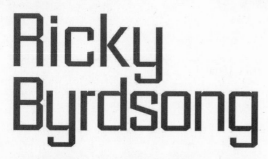

Ricky Byrdsong

with **Dave** and **Neta** Jackson

foreword by **Lute Olson**

BETHANY HOUSE PUBLISHERS
Minneapolis, Minnesota 55438

Coaching Your Kids in the Game of Life
by Ricky Byrdsong with Dave and Neta Jackson

Copyright © 2000
The estate of Ricky Byrdsong

Cover design by Kochel Peterson & Associates

Published by Bethany House Publishers
A Ministry of Bethany Fellowship International
11400 Hampshire Avenue South
Bloomington, Minnesota 55438
www.bethanyhouse.com

Printed in the United States of America by
Bethany Press International, Bloomington, Minnesota 55438

Library of Congress Cataloging-in-Publication Data

Byrdsong, Ricky, d. 1999
    Coaching your kids in the game of life / by Ricky Byrdsong; with Dave and Neta Jackson.
        p.   cm.
Includes bibliographical references (p.   ).
    ISBN 0-7642-2353-4 (hard: alk. paper)
    ISBN 0-7642-2445-X (pbk.)
    1. Child rearing. 2. Parenting. 3. Parent and child.
    I. Jackson, Dave. II. Jackson, Neta. III. Title.
HQ769 B94 2000
G49'.1—dc21

                                         00-008001

In Memory of Ricky Byrdsong

On July 2, 1999, Ricky Byrdsong was tragically murdered by a white supremacist on a two-state killing rampage. Ricky had been working on this book for nearly two years and had finished more than half of it before his death.

Through the diligent efforts of Dave and Neta Jackson, the balance of the book was completed from Ricky's tapes and notes and numerous interviews. Ricky's wife, Sherialyn, gave invaluable assistance to make sure the book reflected Ricky's heart.

It is our hope and prayer that Ricky's message will touch many hearts and change the lives of many families.

Bethany House Publishers

ACKNOWLEDGMENTS

From start to finish, this book has been a team effort. Our heartfelt thanks go to . . .

Patrick Ryan, chairman and CEO of the Aon Corporation, who saw in Ricky a man who would be an asset to his team, and said, "I want to support your book project." As Ricky's coauthors, we were awed that Pat Ryan was willing to fund us, sight unseen, on Ricky's word alone. Thanks for your trust. Also, *John Roskopf*, vice president of financial relations, who was our contact person at Aon after Ricky's death; and *Al Porteus*, director of creative services, who went out of his way to provide pictures of Ricky from Aon's archives, even delivering them in person.

Pastor Lyle Foster, Ricky's and our pastor at The Worship Center in Evanston, Illinois, who was a constant source of encouragement to "Coach" (as he always called Ricky) and willing to brainstorm ideas at odd hours. It was Pastor Lyle who suggested that Coach and we get together to talk about this book. It was Pastor Lyle who proclaimed, "Love is stronger than hate," when a hate-filled shooter went on a rampage that ended Ricky's life. Thanks, Pastor, for your many notes, calls, prayers, and words of encouragement to us as we struggled to finish Ricky's project without him.

Pastor Haman Cross Jr. of Rosedale Park Baptist Church in Detroit, Michigan. Pastor Cross always motivated Ricky to set goals that would s-t-r-e-t-c-h him, to dream big and work hard, and to never give up. Ricky considered Pastor Cross as one of his top "assistant coaches," someone that he would consult with during "time-outs" to get his input and learn from his wisdom and experience.

The many coaches in Ricky's life who believed in him and helped to make him the man and coach that he was: William Lester, Larry Cart, Donald Dollar, Jim Lewis, Lynn Nance, Les Wothke, Steve Fisher, Rick Samuels, Ben Lindsey, Jim Crews, Bobby Knight, and Lute Olson.

Mary Jasper, Ricky's mother, who blessed her only son with unconditional and sacrificial love throughout his life. Mary is the epitome of a loving and devoted mother, who selflessly gives to her children. She was a constant source of encouragement and support to her son.

Marcia Byrdsong, Ricky's sister, who was an endless source of support and encouragement. Marcia often called to check up on her big brother, always willing to be a listening ear and willing to do whatever she could to make this book a reality and a success.

Blanche Hollis, Ricky's grandmother, who helped to raise him and taught him about character . . . and was his number one fan.

Steve Laube, senior nonfiction editor at Bethany House Publishers, who called to say Bethany House wanted this book even before he'd finished reading the proposal . . . and two weeks later, when he heard the devastating news that Ricky Byrdsong had been murdered, said, "We're still committed to publishing his book." Thanks, Steve. Thanks, Bethany. Our many years of partnership formed a good foundation to sustain us through all the uncertainty.

Shawn Parrish, former Northwestern University assistant coach under Ricky (now a sales representative for NewsBank), and *Shon Morris*, assistant athletic director at Northwestern University, who not only let us pick their brains and pick their files for details of Coach Byrdsong's tenure at Northwestern but also called to say, "Anything else we can do?"

Gina Behrens, athletic academic advisor at DePaul University. About a month after Coach was killed, we received a fax, out of the blue, from someone we didn't know. Our jaws dropped. It was several pages, titled, "Byrdsong Chapter Notes." Included were notes for the "missing" chapters. It felt like a gift from God. Our "angel" turned out to be a former associate and friend of Coach Byrdsong, who had typed up notes of a brainstorming session she and Coach had had a year earlier. Thanks, Gina, for giving us three phone numbers where we could reach you and for "talking basketball" with us at all hours.

Neil Milbert and *Fred Mitchell*, sportswriters at the *Chicago Tribune*, and *Bruce Pascoe* of the *Arizona Daily Star*, who graciously fielded our calls and dug up details on sports events. We have a new respect for your profession and your professionalism.

The Worship Center family, who loved Coach like a brother and took on his book project as if it were their own.

And last but not least, *Sherialyn Byrdsong*, Ricky's wife of twenty years. Ricky was deeply grateful to Sherialyn for being his loyal and committed partner in coaching their kids together in the game of life. Her example as a wife and mother served as an inspiration and role model to him in writing this book. Sherialyn, we too are grateful to you, not only for giving us your time and wisdom to make sure this book reflected Ricky's heart but also for teaching us what courage, grace, and faith really mean. You and Ricky have changed our lives.

We feel deeply privileged to have had a part in helping to make Ricky Byrdsong's dream become a reality.

Dave and Neta Jackson
Evanston, Illinois

RICKY BYRDSONG spent eighteen years as a college basketball coach and is best known for his head coaching position with the Northwestern University Wildcats. Tragically, Ricky's life was ended in a drive-by shooting on July 2, 1999, near his home in Evanston, Illinois, where he lived with his wife, Sherialyn, and their three children.

DAVE and NETA JACKSON are award-winning writers of over seventy books. Since starting Castle Rock Creative, Inc., in 1986, they have divided their time between desktop publishing, coauthoring books, and writing their own books. They attend the same church as the Byrdsongs in Illinois.

CONTENTS

FOREWORD

Ricky Byrdsong was a very special person to nearly everyone he met. His smile could light up a room. His personality was one of unbelievable depth.

Ricky never met a stranger. A stranger was a friend to be met.

Ricky had a feel for people that surpassed anyone I have ever known. His commonsense approach to life was legendary among people who knew him well. My family and I felt blessed to have had him as part of our lives for six years while he was one of my assistants at the University of Arizona.

Ricky has written a book, *Coaching Your Kids in the Game of Life*, that allows you to share in this "Gentle Giant's" commonsense approach to life. In it he provides insights into how you can become a "coach" in raising your kids to equal the John Woodens and Dean Smiths of this world. He also emphasizes the importance of having a staff that can provide the necessary leadership to assist in helping the "players" develop to their full potential so that they too can become productive members of society. Ricky's experiences as a player, a coach, and a father will enlighten your life, as they have mine, and allow you to become an all-star coach to your kids.

—Lute Olson
head basketball coach
University of Arizona

INTRODUCTION

The day Coach Lester called me out changed my life forever.

I remember it like it was yesterday. Tenth grade. Frederick Douglass High School in Atlanta. Between classes. Tall and gangly for my age, I was pushing my way through the crowded hallway in the nonchalant don't-look-like-you're-hurrying-but-don't-be-late-for-your-next-class gait that characterized all the boys my age.

All of a sudden, a big booming voice pealed like a thunderclap behind me: "Hey, son!"

Every male in that school hallway shrank into his shirt collar. We all knew who it was: Coach Lester. He was a big 6' 4" barrel-chested man, and whenever his thunderous voice rolled down the hallway, everybody stopped mid-stride. Besides being the basketball coach, he also had a reputation for being the school disciplinarian. So when we heard him yell, everyone in the hall froze and looked warily in his direction. The first thing we thought was *Uh-oh, somebody's in trouble.* He had our attention.

He fixed me with his piercing eyes and bellowed, "Yeah, you, son!"

I pointed at myself and gave him my best innocent "Who, me?" look.

"Yeah, *you,* son!"

Weak-kneed, I started walking toward him. *Oh my, what have I done?* I didn't *think* I'd been having any problems with anyone recently. What teacher had a beef with me and turned me in to Coach Lester?

Everyone in the hall was staring. They all wanted to know why I was in trouble with "the man."

I stopped in front of him, my 6' 5" frame trembling in my shoes.

"Son . . ." he said, looking me up and down. I was standing right in front of him, but his voice was so big it still sounded like he was shouting. "You're too big to be walking these halls and not playing basketball!" Then after a moment he said, "I'll see you in the gym at 3:30 . . . *today*."

Whew! That was *all*? Then suddenly what he had said sank in. "But Coach!" I sputtered. "I've never played basketball."

"Did you hear what I said? I'll see you at 3:30!"

"But Coach! I don't have any basketball clothes . . . I don't have any shoes—"

"I'll see you at 3:30!" And he walked away.

At lunchtime I made a beeline for the pay phone. "Ma! The coach stopped me in the hall and told me I'm going out for basketball."

She said, "You don't know anything about playing basketball."

"I told him that! But he just said I better be there at 3:30 *today*."

"But, Ricky, you don't have any clothes; you don't have any gym shoes—"

"Ma, I told him all that! He *said*, be there at 3:30."

It wasn't just my mother, either. All day long my friends were telling me, "You don't know anything about basketball, Byrdsong."

And I agreed! "I know, man, but what am I supposed to do? He told me to be there at 3:30! I gotta go out." Frankly, at that point I was less scared of what would happen on the basketball floor than of what would happen if I didn't report for practice and ran into Coach Lester the next day.

So I went.

And from that day to this, there has never been a question in my mind that everything that has happened to me—becoming a basketball player, then a coach, raising my own three kids, having a desire to do this book—was born that day when Coach called me out and said, "Hey, son! Yes, you! You can do it!"

Coach Lester did that day what all of us parents need to do for our kids: he made me understand the importance of being part of a team with a purpose. He gave me vision: "This is what you're capable of doing." Then he said, "And I'm going to help you do it."

Up until that time, I had never been a troublemaker, but I was drifting. I had no idea what my goals were or where I was headed. My mom, like many parents—especially single parents—really didn't have time to think about those things. She was working double shifts just to make ends meet, trying to survive, trying to put food on the table. Her goals were pretty basic: "I don't want Ricky on drugs, and I don't want him running with the wrong crowd."

Had Coach Lester not called me out and given me direction, I might have stayed out of trouble, but . . . for what? I didn't have anything positive to shoot for, nothing I was striving to become. At some point, I might have said, "What am I preserving my 'goodness' for?"

Coach Lester helped me to see the bigger picture.

I remember when he told me, "You can get a college scholarship."

College? The guy was crazy! I was saying, "But I don't know how, I don't have it."

He kept saying, "Yes, you do. I'm going to show you; I'm going to work with you. You can do it."

And he was right. I knew it the day I set foot on a college campus, scholarship in hand. He believed in me. Maybe he thought more of me than I deserved, but I knew I couldn't let him down.

Many times since the day I heard that big voice bellow, *"Hey, son!"* I've thought, *If only every kid had a Coach Lester to call him out, to believe in him, give him a goal, work with him to help him reach his potential—what a difference it would make.* When I drive around now and see kids hanging out on the street corner, I pick one out of the crowd and think, *Man! If someone could just do for you what Coach Lester did for me.* Because that kid doesn't have to end up hanging around the street corner . . . or in prison . . . or in the morgue. What if, at a critical point in his life, someone would say, "Hey, son! Come here! You can do . . . whatever! I'll see you today at 3:30." That kid would be there, and it would change his life.

But there aren't enough coaches to go around.

For eighteen years, while I was coaching college basketball, I often heard people say, "Hey, Coach. Your coaching looks a lot like parenting." Having three kids of my own, I knew it was true. My responsibilities as a coach were to inspire and to equip my players to achieve their dreams. The game of basketball was only a means for preparing my players for a bigger and more important game—the game of life.

That's my job as a parent too. You may not know anything about coaching, but I'm hoping this book will turn you into a good one. Parents—as the family "coach"—need to create a team with a purpose. They need to "call out" their kids, give them a vision for who they can be and what they can do, and then equip them to do it.

Every kid needs a Coach Lester. In your family that "coach" is you.

Because life is a game that no one can afford to lose.

1. "I LOVE THIS GAME!"

Graduation. You know what it feels like. You're tired, you're excited—you're glad to be done with exams! On the one hand you're thinking, *I'm outta here*. And on the other you feel kind of jittery: *Man, now I gotta do something. But what?*

At least that's how I felt as I approached college graduation in 1978. I had played basketball for two years at Iowa State University while I finished my degree in communications. Then, just as I was about to close that door behind me, I got a message that Coach Lynn Nance wanted to see me.

Approaching his office, I felt a little nervous. Why would he want to see me? The season was over. I'd done well for the Cyclones, but, hey, I was graduating, heading out to who-knows-where. Had I done something wrong? I didn't think so. He probably just wanted to say good-bye. Tough as he was, I knew he'd send me off with a good word.

I poked my head in the door of an office that was replete with plaques and photos of players who had gone on to the NBA. "Sit down," he said. He rocked back in his old leather chair, and with his fingers laced behind his thick, curly brown hair, he got right to the point.

"How'd you like to be my assistant coach?"

I had to stifle an urge to look around. I knew there was no one else in his office, but he couldn't possibly mean *me*! I was just a college kid . . . who'd never coached before. I pointed to the floor. "Here?" I asked, thinking he must mean somewhere else; maybe he'd come across a grade school job and was tossing it my way simply because I had played the game.

"You heard me. Right here at Iowa State, as my number-three assistant. You interested?"

"Wow!" I pulled myself up a little straighter in the chair. "Excuse me for asking," I said, "but . . . why would you offer me a job on your staff when I've had no experience whatsoever?"

He stared at me so long that I thought I'd blown it with my impertinent question. Finally he said without a flicker in his steely expression, "Two things: I know you love the game, and I believe you'd be loyal to me. Am I right?"

"Well, yeah. Of course." I laughed nervously, then worried that my laugh made me sound like the kid I was.

Today, after eighteen years of coaching, I know Coach Nance put his finger on two crucial qualities that make for an effective coaching staff. He was laying a solid foundation for the kind of team he wanted to build, and it started with his staff.

A lot of adults don't bring any more to the task of parenting than *love* and *loyalty*, but those crucial elements are as important to parenting as they are to coaching. One doesn't need to be perfect, but to succeed one must be ready to learn. Love and loyalty create a teachable spirit for the task at hand. And with a teachable spirit, the other requirements for a successful coach—or parent—can be learned.

In this chapter, I will talk about you, the "coaching staff," and the foundations that are required to build an effective family team. In the next chapter, I'll talk about how your relationship with your spouse affects your ability to "coach." We'll work on how you can improve both your foundation and your relationships. As we look at some of these fundamentals, you may be tempted to say, "Let's get on with the coaching. I need some help with my kids!" But be patient. The fundamentals are as essential in the game of life as they are in basketball.

1. THE FOUNDATION

Man, I love this game!

Catching that pass, dribbling down the court, faking out your opponent, taking the jumper, hearing the ball go *swish!* followed by the roar of the crowd . . . now that's a real adrenaline rush. But there's more to really loving the game than feeling that high.

Coach Nance tested my love of the game when I first joined his team. I came to Iowa State from Pratt Junior College in Kansas, where I had been a two-time all-conference guard and team captain . . . but that merely gave me the opportunity to be among the thirty-five people trying out for the Cyclones. When I arrived on campus, he asked me, along with all the other wannabes: "Do you love this game?"

And, like everyone else, I said, "Yes, I love the game!"

"OK," he said. "Report tomorrow at 5:30 A.M."

Did he say 5:30 A.M.? He did. And we showed up. We ran 220-yard dashes until we dropped, and then we hit the gym to lift weights until our exploding muscles screamed for mercy. Then he ran us out on the floor to practice the "basics." Finally we got to go back out into the fresh air and run some more 220s. Before we got too cold, though, Coach hustled us back into the nice warm weight room to pump more iron.

By the end of the day, we were all grumbling, "What does all this have to do with basketball?"

Coach Nance feigned surprise. "I thought you guys said you loved the game."

"Hey, we do, we do," we all said. But a lot of the guys were already making other plans.

Jabbing his finger at us, the no-nonsense former FBI agent said, "Let's get one thing straight. Loving the game ain't no warm fuzzy feeling. It's not hearing the ball go swish, it's not hearing the crowd scream when you make a basket, it's not a trip to Hawaii to play a tournament game. It's being willing to do *whatever it takes* to become a successful team, and often that's more difficult than your conscious mind thinks possible."

The next day those thirty-five

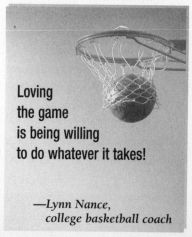

Loving
the game
is being willing
to do whatever it takes!

—Lynn Nance,
college basketball coach

wannabes, all of whom said, "I love the game," had dwindled to seventeen teachable potential teammates—not much different than the ratio between those who say, "I love you, babe!" at the altar and then quit in divorce.[1]

Gymnast Jennifer Pappalardo exemplifies this kind of love for the game. By the time she became a junior in high school, she had undergone six painful operations on her ankle, most of them necessitated by her participation on the Lions gymnastics team of Lyons, Illinois. But she kept on competing. Why was she willing to undergo that much pain? Because the Lions, who placed fifth in the state the year before, had set a goal for themselves to win first place in 1999. Pappalardo, who helped her team score 149.05 in 1998–99, said, "That's what we want more than ever. It is real important to us to come away with a trophy. . . . I can't think of anything else I would like to do more. I love it that much."[2]

That's love of the game.

Some people might question that kind of love, that kind of commitment to a mere sport. But as a coach, I've seen how sports can teach us a lot about life and about the kind of love and loyalty that builds a strong family team.

Do you have the kind of love for your family that will see you through six (or even more) excruciatingly painful experiences without quitting? Are you willing to do whatever it takes to be a successful team?

2. COMMITMENT

Jennifer Pappalardo's love of gymnastics led her to a commitment to the sport, one that carried her through sacrifice and even suffering. There were probably many times when she didn't *feel* like continuing. That's when she had to reach down deep and call on her commitment. In sports, as in most areas of life, when commitments reach a certain level, they are formalized.

When players go professional, there's always a contract. When I became a coach, there was a contract. At that stage, other people's well-being depended on my fulfilling certain expectations . . . even if

---

[1]"Birth, Marriage, Divorce, and Deaths for July 28, 1998," *Monthly Vital Statistics Report*, vol. 46, no. 12 (Hyattsville, Maryland: National Center for Health Statistics, 1998). The ratio of one divorce for every two marriages has remained relatively constant since 1980.

[2]Dick Quagliano, "Healthy Pappalardo Boosts Lyons Gymnasts," *Chicago Sun-Times*, January 15, 1999, 105.

tremendous pressures developed for me to do something different.

When NBA coaches are hired, for instance, they typically sign a contract that commits them exclusively to a team until the season is over. Assistant coaches at this level easily make six figures. But head coaches can make millions a year—several times that of assistant coaches. Obviously the ambition of most assistant coaches is to land a head coaching position. However, a dilemma sometimes arises when the regular season

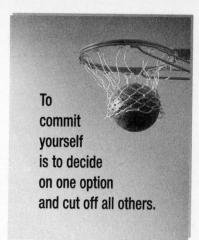

To commit yourself is to decide on one option and cut off all others.

ends and teams are looking for a new head coach. Any team that needs a new head coach can approach anyone in the league with an offer—anyone, that is, except the assistant coaches of the playoff teams (who are sometimes the most attractive because of their record). *Their* season has *not* ended. They are still under contract and cannot legally begin bargaining for a new job. So here's where the pressure mounts: Do they comply with the constraints of their contracts, or do they negotiate under the table to land one of the highly coveted head coaching positions before the opportunities disappear? The incentive of an $800,000-a-year raise may tempt some to break the rules, but if a professional team is going to have any real success, the coaching staff must have committed, or *decided*, back at contract time, to stay together for the duration, no matter what. Interestingly, the Latin root of "decide" is *decidere*, literally "to cut off all other possibilities."

That's the meaning of commitment—to cut off all other possibilities.

My mom was the one who first taught me this. Many times she worked a double shift, either on the assembly line at Nabisco or at her job at K-Mart. They weren't fun jobs, and she could have quit at any time. But she didn't. Because of her commitment to the family—our team—she hung in there. Nothing could knock her out of the box. She was a single mother, and there were times when "other possibilities" presented themselves, but she had a commitment to our family. Had she been thinking only of herself, some new relationships might have been attractive to her. But she cut herself off from them because she knew they would have interfered with her mission for us as a family.

Was her sacrifice worth it? I think so. Because that was the very thing that kept me from quitting when it felt like Coach Nance was killing us. Oh, yeah, I wanted to quit! But how would I have ever faced Mom? I couldn't imagine dragging myself home and saying, "It was just too tough for me"—not after what she went through to get me there. Her example led to my career. What is your example likely to produce in your children?

Our next-door neighbors have been married for approximately forty years. Recently, when my wife and I visited their home for a friendly gathering, out of curiosity we asked them what their secret was. We thought they might give us the ABC's of good communication, or tell us about the importance of choosing a compatible mate in the first place, or explain to us the mystery of compromise.

Instead, they looked knowingly at each other and said, "We've had our rough times. In fact, we faced some tremendous challenges—the kinds of things that have broken up a lot of other marriages—but we simply decided to hang in there. And now we're reaping the rewards."

Hang in there.

That's it?

Of course, there are some important things to build into your family so that it's not just "hanging in there" by the skin of your teeth. But sometimes to get to those things, to have the courage to work on those things, we have to hang in there in order to get through the rough places and out the other side.

Hanging in there often requires outside support—counseling or encouragement from trustworthy friends. In my own marriage, it's what has kept my wife, Sherialyn, and me together. The arrival of our three children, Sabrina, Kelley, and Ricky Jr., brought a dynamic we were not prepared for, and had it not been for the counsel of wise pastors from our church, we probably would have joined the ranks of the divorced.

But you have to be careful whose counsel you seek. So-called friends who only commiserate with you may make you feel good for a time, but, in the end, they don't have to pay the price. As a coach, I remember calling Jim Crews, the head coach at Evansville University, because I was totally frustrated with a couple of my players and didn't know what to do. He said, "Well, what are you going to do to make your relationship with them better?" I guess I had hoped he would say it was all right to boot them off the team. But he didn't let me off that easily. Even when I said that I had done all I could, he said, "No way. There's always one more thing you can do. So try it, and then call me."

That's the kind of friend we need when we're struggling in our marriage.

What is your level of commitment? Have you decided to keep your "coaching staff" together until the mission is accomplished? Have you decided to pursue your mission for your family, no matter what? Believe me, you won't be able to do it if you toy with the other possibilities. You've got to *decide*; you've got to cut off all other possibilities!

Some people downplay the value of sports in our society. To them it's just "playing games," and there's no doubt that sports is far out of balance for many people. Nevertheless, it remains a bastion of certain values that sadly have fallen out of favor in much of our culture. Who is it that tells you, "No pain, no gain"? The coach. Almost everyone else, from the multimedia advertiser to the psychotherapist, will suggest there's an easier way to get what you want. Hey, I'd be as delighted as the next guy if my car would go a hundred thousand miles without a tune-up. But you and I know it's not going to happen. The no pain, no gain maxim is as true today as it was when our ancestors were bustin' clods to get a crop.

It's natural for kids to seek the easy way out—to avoid homework, tell a white lie, steal the leather jacket, change their moods with chemicals, but if you want to coach them in how to achieve true happiness and lasting values, you will have to demonstrate commitment.

3. ESTABLISHING THE MISSION

On a basketball team, every player needs to focus on something greater than himself or herself. At Iowa State, even after we made the team, Coach Nance often asked us, "Why do you want to be on this team?" He knew that many new players had the fantasy of becoming famous, the big man on campus. Others dreamed of becoming rich by making it to the NBA. But neither of those goals was good from the coach's point of view. Neither focused on what was good for the team. Our love for the game could not be for selfish rewards. We needed a vision adjustment. We had to embrace a mission that would help the whole team prosper.

This principle became so important for me that, as the head coach for the Northwestern University Wildcats, I drafted a formal mission statement for my players (see appendix B). But at this point I want to focus on refining the mission of the staff, which, in the case of the family, is the husband and wife. For those of you who are single parents,

Where there is no vision, the people perish.

—Proverbs 29:18

the "staff" is primarily you.

When two people get married, they need to have some idea of what their purpose is for coming together. However intense their love for one another might be, if their purpose is primarily selfish, they will be shaken when the tough times come. If you are a single parent, your mission has to be just as focused. You don't have time to waste your energy and resources drifting from one interest to another. I think the *vision* or *mission statement* ought to apply to the whole family, and it should be simple enough that even very young members can understand it.

For instance, the mission statement for our family is very simple:

> The mission of the Byrdsong family is to make our world
> a better place by helping others to fulfill God's plan for
> their lives so that God will say to us when we see Him,
> "Well done, my good and faithful servants."

Everything we do centers around this. I also prepared a more specific mission statement for my children (see appendix A). We'll discuss its value in chapter 3, but even this more simple family statement applies to the kids. When my eight-year-old son, Ricky, says, "Dad, I want to be rich," I don't pour cold water on that desire, I merely nudge him to see it in terms of our family mission statement. How will his becoming rich make society a better place and cause God to say, "Well done"? The statement doesn't dictate what the kids will do in terms of their careers or where they will live or who they will marry. Instead, it focuses on character.

A mission statement helps you stay on course and corrects you when you stray. When a basketball player is tempted to stay out late at night or to not take good care of his body, the mission statement reminds him that he is committed to the team's goal and not to selfish gratification. Without a clear understanding of that purpose, other interests can quickly take over.

The same is true in marriage. Too often young couples enthusiastically marry without agreeing on a goal outside themselves. They are drawn together by the promise of self-gratification. Now, don't get me wrong! I'm all in favor of marriage being gratifying for each partner. But if they have not jointly agreed on a higher purpose, the day may come when their individual interests will detract from and ultimately threaten the marriage. One may say, "This marriage isn't helping me realize my goals to become an architect" or "My marriage is too confining. I'm sure I'd be more fulfilled in another relationship."

> Obviously there have been times when I've failed. But there have never been times when I thought I would fail.
>
> —*Michael Jordan,*
> *NBA star*

I'm not saying *what* your family's mission statement should be, only that each family should have one. In *The 7 Habits of Highly Effective People*, Habit 2 says, "Begin With the End in Mind."[3] It goes on to state that all things are created twice, first in the mind and then in reality. Endeavors that fail, fail in the first creation, often because the purpose was not adequately refined. The most effective way to begin with the end in mind is to develop a mission statement.

It is the focusing quality of your mission statement that will help you as a family make small decisions by some method other than default—e.g., how much time you should spend taxiing the kids around to soccer practice or gymnastics; whether or not they watch the same music videos and play the same video games as everyone else does; whether curfews are archaic. But your mission statement should also help you to make the big decisions, like whether or not to accept the job offer that requires the family to move across the country.

4. ARE YOU A FIT PARENT?

Usually when people think of sports and fitness, they think only of the physical fitness of the players. When they think of parenting and fitness, they usually think of its moral or emotional aspects.

It has been my observation, however, that good parenting—like good coaching—requires all three: physical fitness, moral fitness, and emo-

---

[3]Stephen R. Covey, *The 7 Habits of Highly Effective People* (New York: Simon & Schuster, 1989).

tional fitness. But parenting is an exhausting business, so in this chapter I want to deal with the foundation of being physically fit for the job.

In coaching, we recruit players who already have talent. We know they can pass, shoot, and dribble or we wouldn't even look at them. But when they report for the team, our first task is to get them physically fit to use those abilities. Coaches understand that the foundation of any success—regardless of talent or desire—is the energy to see the task through to completion.

Coaches don't institute curfews just to squelch their players' fun. They don't watch how they eat because they are trying to be their mamas. And they don't require endless physical workouts because they are sadistic. They do these things because physical fitness is foundational to success. A well-known saying in sports is, "Fatigue makes cowards of us all!" If a player is tired when facing a stiff challenge, he'll run from it. He'll unconsciously position himself out of the action or pass the ball when he should drive hard through the lane for the hoop.

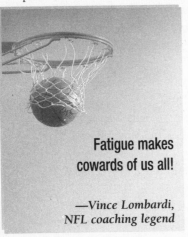

Fatigue makes cowards of us all!

—Vince Lombardi, NFL coaching legend

He'll only jump three times for a rebound when his opponent goes up a fourth time . . . and comes down with the ball.

When we are tired, we shrink from even *trying* the challenge because the energy just isn't there.

Parenting is no exception. We may have all the tools, know how to communicate with kids, love them, and desire to raise them effectively, but if we don't understand the necessity of being physically fit, we are in danger of failing simply for lack of energy. How fit do you have to be? Fit enough so that you aren't shrinking from your duties because you are too tired.

When our kids come home from school and need help with their homework, if we're just barely dragging ourselves around, we end up saying things like "Don't bother me right now" or "Try to figure it out yourself."

Too often the relationships or interests our kids develop outside the home—and that scare us—can be traced back to their efforts to engage us when we were too tired to respond. More than once when my kids asked me to go out and play so they could learn how to catch or shoot baskets, I put them off—until one day I realized they weren't asking anymore. They were either doing those things with other kids or had lost interest and turned to Nintendo or something else. Suddenly I was saying, "Hey, let's go play catch," but I had lost my opportunity, because when the time was ripe I had been too tired.

The same thing happens in marriage. Too often we are just too tired to talk, too tired to listen, too tired to even want to think about it. Frustration and lack of good communication coincide with being too tired.

I understand when parents say, "I'm just too tired right now." Parents don't make that up, but we are the ones responsible for changing the situation. We must ask ourselves what is necessary to recover the required energy. If we are running low on gas in our car, the only option if we want to keep going is to put more gas in the tank. Physically we do that for our bodies with a proper diet, adequate sleep, and sufficient exercise. And that's what's needed if you are going to be a good parent.

There was a time when I realized that I didn't have enough "gas in my tank" to fulfill the reasonable and important expectations of my family. I had slipped into a pattern of coming home a little late—often after the family had begun supper. I was tired when I came in, so after greeting everyone, I went upstairs and changed from my suit and tie into something a little more comfortable. Then I'd wash up and sit down to read the paper for a few minutes just to unwind. When I was ready, I'd come down to join the family. By then they had usually finished the meal, and the kids had scattered.

I noticed that Sherialyn seemed irritated with me, so I probed until I discovered that she was at her wits' end over my evening routine. Being at the supper table *with* the family was important, and I was blowing it off. Of course, I tried to justify my actions by saying that I was tired and deserved a window of relaxation before I engaged in the reports from school and Ricky telling on Kelley and Kelley telling on Sabrina. I just didn't need that the minute I walked in the door. But the look on her face didn't change, and when I thought about it, I knew she was right. I was facing a fitness issue.

So I changed my routine. I needed to get home a little earlier so I could be present and ready for the suppertime interaction. I also needed to get to bed a little earlier at night so I wouldn't be so tired at the end of the day. I also got back into an exercise routine because I knew that really adds to one's overall energy, and it's been working. The adjustment definitely helped!

The needs of our families don't revolve around our convenience or our readiness to meet them. Their needs are constant and so should be our readiness. That means keeping fit, and there's no other way to accomplish this than by proper diet, adequate rest, and plenty of exercise.

INSTANT REPLAY

Ten years after I began my coaching career at Iowa State, I landed my first head coaching job at the University of Detroit Mercy. My first task was to put together my coaching staff. Over one hundred applications landed on my desk the first day, and that didn't even count the former assistants who met me at the door saying, "Hi, Coach. Do I still have a job?"

Some of the applicants mailed in their résumés, some tried to phone them in, and some drove great distances to hand them to me in person, hoping for a few minutes of my time. Every one began with, "Here's what my record is. Here's what I've accomplished. I've coached such and such number of years."

But then there was a local applicant who came into my office really wanting the job who had something different to say. His name was Scott Perry.

"Where are you coaching right now?" I asked.

"I've never coached," he admitted. "I work in a bank."

I don't even want to tell you what my first thought was. But I resisted the urge to show him the door and asked more about his background. He had played basketball at Wayne State University in Detroit, but then he went into the business world for two years. So why was he applying for a coaching job? I was ready to dismiss him right there, but then I remembered that I, too, had never coached when I got my first job. So I said, "What do you think you can bring to this program?"

"I love the game, Coach," he said, "and no one will be more loyal than I will."

Bingo! I stopped shuffling through the other applications and looked at him carefully for the first time. Where'd he come up with a line like that?

"Let me think about this for a while," I said. "I'll get back to you."

His references—and a few I sleuthed out myself—all confirmed his claims: even though this guy lacked experience, he brought the foundational qualities I wanted in my coaching staff. Ultimately I hired him. Coach Nance had set me straight: start with a solid foundation and a trustworthy relationship, and many of the other skills can be mastered. Scott developed into a fine coach. In fact, today he is the head basketball coach at Eastern Kentucky University.

You have the same potential if you begin with a solid foundation and pay attention to the relationship with your "coaching staff." In our next chapter, we'll look at why that relationship is so critical to *coaching your kids in the game of life* and how you can improve it—beginning with the quality of *loyalty*.

FREE THROW

1. Write a one-paragraph statement of your commitment to your spouse and to your family

Be honest. Are there any qualifiers? Discuss your commitment with your spouse.

2. Write a mission statement for your family

Step 1—State who you are.

"We . . ."

Step 2—State what you want to do.

"will . . ."

Step 3—State how you plan to do it.

"by . . ."

Step 4—State your compelling reason.

"so that . . ."

Notice how the Byrdsong family mission statement fulfills these four steps: (1) *The mission of the Byrdsong family* (2) *is to make our world a better place* (3) *by helping others to fulfill God's plan for their lives* (4) *so that God will say to us when we see Him, "Well done, my good and faithful servants."*

Try to keep your family mission statement between twenty-five and eighty words. Refine it until it expresses what you and your spouse consider most important for your family. It should work like a magnifying glass does on the sun's rays: focusing everyone's energy without filtering out anyone's potential.

3. Evaluate your own physical "fitness" as a parent

How often do you find yourself saying to your spouse or kids, "Not now. I'm too tired"? Do you have the energy to "plan ahead" or do you just "react" to whatever comes up? Take three small steps toward fitness:

- Are you getting enough sleep? Try going to bed half an hour earlier.
- Are you getting enough exercise? Add a thirty-minute vigorous walk to your day—at your lunchtime, running an errand, or walking the dog.
- Are you eating on the run? Cut out the snacks, eat a "starter" breakfast, make suppertime family time.

2. PLAYING FOR KEEPS WITH YOUR STAFF

When Coach Nance offered me a job as assistant coach at Iowa State and said he believed that I would be loyal to him, I wasn't sure what he meant. Who or what might test my loyalty? Still scratching my head, I snagged Reggie Warford, one of the other assistant coaches, and in the course of rejoicing over my new job, I did a little investigating.

"Hey, Reggie. Coach Nance said he knew that I loved the game, and I do! But he also said he knew I would be loyal. It was a big deal to him, but—" I lowered my voice. "What's he expecting?"

"Bottom line," said Reggie, "remaining in agreement with him in public. Look, Byrdsong, there may be times when you don't understand or agree with what he is doing. And there might not be time for him to explain himself to your satisfaction. Occasionally you might even be right! Nevertheless, the success of the team depends on the players' confidence in Coach Nance's direction. If you undermine that, you not only undermine Coach's authority, you could shake the whole team and destroy our chance for success."

I gulped, not because I didn't think Coach Nance was the greatest, but because it sounded like I was being asked to be a yes-man. As the old saying goes, "If two people always agree, one of them isn't necessary." I didn't want that fate.

So what did loyalty *really* mean? And why was it so important to developing a good coaching staff? I soon found out.

1. LOYALTY MATTERS

Now that I was on the sidelines with the coaches instead of on the floor with the players, I couldn't believe how many complaints we got about the coaching! Sometimes they came from the fans, sometimes from the alumni, sometimes from the media. And just like a kid trying to get one parent to side against the other, people came to me and asked if I didn't think a different approach would have been better.

But Reggie had warned me. "That's when loyalty matters, Byrdsong. Even if you think a different play—maybe one you had in mind—might have won the game, you need to convince the critics that your support is clearly behind the decision Coach Nance made. Later, in private, possibly in a staff meeting," he said, "you can respectfully test your ideas, but never in public. And *respectfully* is the operative term. Even in private, don't come on like you know it all. Don't cling to your opinion, unwilling to be swayed."

Respectfully test ideas in private, but never oppose your staff partner in public.

Reggie also sketched out what would happen if I *did* air my differences in public: "The media and other critics would be all over you like ants at a picnic! They'd treat you like honey for a time, but their only interest would be to bring down Coach Nance, and the result would divide the team. That's what loyalty is all about!"

I got the picture.

Reggie was right, and it wasn't too long before my loyalty was put to the test. Coach Nance hailed from Kentucky. When he recruited a young man by the name of Bob Fowler from his home state and ended up making him a starting player, the situation was ripe for some of the other players to wonder whether favoritism was operating here. Coach Nance was white, and I was black, so it was natural for some of the black players on the team to ask me whether I thought Coach Nance was favoring his "home boy," who was also white.

The tough part was that I didn't think Fowler had proved himself superior to some of the other players who might have started, so even I wondered whether Coach Nance was acting out of some unconscious favoritism. Nevertheless, when some of the players came to me to validate their feelings, I said, "If you have a problem with what's going on, you need to speak to Coach Nance personally. Coach is fair-minded, and I want you to come to feel that way about him."

This was an honest expression of my loyalty. At the core of my being, I did believe that he was fair-minded. I'm sure he believed Fowler had earned his starting position, even if I hadn't seen it. Therefore, I could make that statement honestly to the players and avoid the potential of splitting the team.

It was good practice for what I was to face later as a father, because in the family loyalty must extend from father to mother as well as from mother to father. For instance, Sherialyn believes that our kids should learn piano to give them a basic foundation in music. At one time or another, they've each wailed about the injustice of it all and appealed to me for relief. Maybe they suspected I didn't think piano was quite as essential as their mom did. And frankly, unless a child proves gifted in piano, I'd probably not push it when he or she became too frustrated. I would probably let the child spend the time practicing what he or she excels in.

But when my kids complain, I don't say, "I agree, but that's what your mom wants." That would undermine both of us. It would undermine her because I would have sided against her, but it would also undermine my authority because it would suggest that I didn't have any say in the matter.

Instead, I say something like, "Sometimes in life we all must do things we don't enjoy, and right now piano practice is one of them for you. One day you'll be glad you put in the time." That's a truthful response, and it gives the message that whether their suspicions about my opinions on practicing are true or not, a higher priority to me is standing in complete unity with my wife. Later, if I really think piano practice needs an adjustment, I can discuss it with her privately until we come to a new agreement.

Loyalty between the parenting "staff" does not mean that you have to pretend you always think alike. You can—and probably should—express your differences in front of your kids on anything that doesn't

A higher priority to me is standing in complete unity with my wife.

have to do with parenting. It's not even harmful for your kids to see you argue— *occasionally*—provided you do it fairly and they see you resolve the dispute. However, when your kids try to use your differences to get around the other parent (and they will!), refuse to play that game. If loyalty is your genuine priority, you'll seldom be caught unaware when it is challenged.

Loyalty is required outside the home as well. Suppose a couple arrives late for dinner, and Hal, the husband, announces, "I'm awfully sorry, but Heather just couldn't get it together tonight." You can be sure the relationship between the "coaching staff" has taken a major hit. In fact, this kind of public sniping is likely to trigger a feud in which the wife looks for an opportunity to say, "Now, Hal, you know you don't need that second piece of cake." Protecting our spouse from public embarrassment builds a strong foundation.

Actually loyalty should characterize all our family relationships. One father of six noted that loyalty to our children is often tested when they are accused of wrongdoing. In an article on family loyalty, he wrote:

> What do I do if an irate neighbor calls to tell me that my boys have put a BB hole in his thermopane door? There is his $300 door, filling with condensation and fogging over forever. Here are my boys, who own BB guns and never could hit the bull's-eye.
>
> The neighbor's report may sound so plausible that I am tempted to summon the boys, chew them out to my neighbor's satisfaction, and announce that they will have to pay for the door from their paper route earnings. The neighbor would be placated and peace restored.
>
> But that wouldn't be loyal to my sons.[1]

The challenge is to balance loyalty to our children with fairness in responding to the one accusing them of wrongdoing. Without assum-

---

[1] Kevin Perrotta, "Family Loyalty," *Growing Together* (Fall 1984): 3:3, 1.

ing that our child is guilty, we can assure the accuser that we will look into the matter thoroughly and get back to him or her. Then we can talk to our child privately. This approach should never insulate our children from taking responsibility for their actions. It merely lets them know that we think and expect the best of them and will stand loyally with them, no matter what.

But besides loyalty, there are some other basics that build a good foundation of unity for the coaching staff, whether on a sports team or in a family.

2. COMMUNICATION IS MORE THAN TALKING

When I first began coaching, I noticed that in our *daily* coaching meetings (sometimes two or three per day), the first thing Coach Nance would say was, "What do you guys think?" He never began by saying, "Here's what we're going to do." His first step in communicating effectively was to listen to us, and he made sure he really understood what we were trying to say too. Sometimes he took notes while we explained our reasoning; then he'd say, "OK, if I've got this right, you think we should do such-and-such for this reason." Sometimes he would test the idea with the other coaches by asking what they thought of the plan, and sometimes he would say, "Well, the problem I see with that is . . ." But he would never say, "That's a dumb idea." Whether our ideas were adopted or not, we always knew that he had taken the time to listen and to understand what we had to say.

Observe to hear. When I became a head coach, I found that communicating effectively was a subject that could fill books (and has), but I also discovered that I was halfway there if I really listened. But listening has to do with far more than merely hearing words. Some of us men don't like to admit that fact. Women may be more intuitive, assigning meaning and innuendo where we didn't intend it—or at least didn't intend to reveal it. We pride ourselves on meaning what we say and saying what we mean, and that's it! We don't want people trying to interpret our tone of voice or our body language. We might even claim we never use body lan-

Coach Nance would never say, "That's a dumb idea."

guage. But think about it: When you walk into a roomful of other men, how they look at you—whether they look at you at all—how they shake your hand, how they maintain their posture, sends messages. You know within minutes whether you are respected, welcomed, and whether others are at ease around you. You quickly sense whether you are going to have to prove yourself.

You pick up these and other messages apart from what anyone says to you. And the other men probably gather similar messages from you. So let's face it, both men and women communicate nonverbally, though possibly over different issues at different times.

Between married partners, nonverbal communication may be even more prevalent than on the job. Research indicates that only 7 percent of what we hear from our spouses involves the words we hear, 38 percent involves tone of voice, and the remaining 55 percent is made up of various nonverbal forms of communication.[2]

Listen to speak. Listening closely to the other person may also give you a clue about how to speak more effectively. Marriage counselor H. Norman Wright says that in most marriages one partner tends to speak in great detail while the other sends cryptic "telegrams." He says there is nothing wrong with either style, but they can frustrate each other. The detail person thinks the other withholds information. The concise person gets tired of the "chatter." However, if you want to be heard better, try using the other person's style.[3]

Wright takes styles of communication one step further and notes that most people think in one of three modes: *visual, auditory,* or *feeling.* The visual person thinks by generating images, even seeing the words of a sentence. They often reveal this pattern in their speech: "I see what you mean." "That looks like a good idea." "You ain't seen nothin' yet." The auditory person uses phrases like, "That sounds good to me." "Tell me more." "I've heard it all." The feeling-oriented person may say, "I sense you're upset." "I'm comfortable with that." "It feels like the right thing."

Of course, no one thinks or speaks exclusively from one orientation, but if you can discern a pattern, try communicating back to your spouse in his or her mode and see if you have more success being heard.[4]

---

[2]Jim Smith, "Getting Things Straight," *Husbands and Wives* (Wheaton, Ill.: Victor Books, 1988), 280.

[3]H. Norman Wright, "Speak Your Partner's Language," *Husbands and Wives* (Wheaton, Ill.: Victor Books, 1988), 289–91.

[4]Ibid.

Meet to agree. Does your "coaching staff" have meetings? Meetings are far more effective than trying to solve problems on the spur of the moment on the court—which, in the family, means at the dinner table with the kids present, on a romantic date, when either of you is about to go out the door, when you are really steamed up, in front of other people, when you are going to bed, or right after either of you have had a hard day. With all those options out of bounds, you will probably have to schedule an actual "talk time." Choose a time and place, and make it regular— at least once a week. You may find that being intentional will relieve the pressure of "He never listens to me" or "I never get a moment's peace."

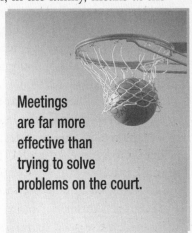

Meetings are far more effective than trying to solve problems on the court.

If at first you can't imagine what needs discussing, set this as your regular agenda:

(a) Review any special events for the coming week.
(b) Discuss any physical needs around the house.
(c) Check on finances.
(d) Consider how the children are doing—child by child.
(e) Inquire seriously about your spouse's well-being:
    "How are you doing?"

Of course, at other times matters will sometimes arise that need immediate attention. However, if it's not an emergency, it is fair to ask, "Can we talk about that at our meeting Thursday night? I'd rather not deal with it right now." And when there are *regular* meetings, it is easier for the other person to agree to wait.

Agree to advance. One of the most important things for "coaches" to remember is to not act independently. Together they constitute a team. One does not make plans or do anything that would surprise the other. This is especially important for maintaining trust and stability between a mother and a father. The *only* surprises that strengthen a marriage are surprise love gifts to each other! Now, of course, many couples have worked out significant divisions of labor and responsibility so that one partner may not know the details of what the other partner decides or does. But those decisions and actions aren't surprises. They are within the arena of delegation.

Anything that exceeds that needs discussion. No wise husband will keep his wife in the dark about anything he plans to do or does—with regard to family money, major direction, significant time, or even his own attitudes and ambitions. The same is true for the wife. Both staff members must keep on the same page. We have to truly agree together in order to advance the family.

Confirm to affirm. I grew up thinking that bringing my wife flowers would be one of the most romantic things I could do for her. But the first time I brought home some roses for Sherialyn, her response was more like, "Oh. That's nice." I felt devastated. My effort fell far short of communicating the affirming message I intended. Finally I discovered that she felt far more affirmed when I cleared off the table or washed the dishes or helped in some other way. If the choice was between "roses" or "help," help won hands down every time. But I had to be told this through a process of communication. If we hadn't talked about it, I would have gone through life thinking she was simply ungrateful for those beautiful roses I brought her.

After we'd been married for a while, we began to take for granted that we knew each other. So we actually stopped talking about things like, "Would you rather have roses or help?" We talked about our jobs or the kids, but not about how to affirm each other. One day I discovered that Sherialyn would like to have gone to a particular concert—which had occurred months before. "Why didn't you say something?" I asked, thinking, *Will I ever understand women?* But she explained that when I came home at night, all I talked about was work and all its pressures so that going to a concert just didn't seem important anymore.

We had fallen out of the habit of taking the time to sit down and confirm that we were still affirming each other in ways that kept our relationship strong and fresh.

Rather than contempt, I think familiarity more often breeds neglect. We get lazy and assume that our spouse is secure in our love. Then one day you realize he or she is not happy and you ask, "What's up?" When your spouse says, "Well, you never tell me you love me" or "We don't do anything together anymore," you finally realize that you've been missing it. We must not take our family "staff" for granted.

3. TAKING RESPONSIBILITY FOR YOUR ROLE

Coaching is a team sport *within* a team sport. In the best of all coaching worlds, a basketball or baseball team has a coaching *staff* to share coaching responsibilities. It's tough on a coach when he or she is responsible not only for representing the team, training the players, and working out game strategy but also recruiting, scouting, and riding herd on the team off the court, all at the same time.

On a well-functioning basketball team, the staff usually consists of the head coach and various assistant coaches. My first role as an assistant coach at Iowa State was recruiter. I had to go out and find the talent that I thought would blend well with the mission we had as a team. Another role given an assistant coach was scouting. This coach went out and scouted the enemy. He brought back valuable information we needed to know if we were going to play the other team well. Another assistant coach's job was to stay on top of the players in the life choices they were making off court that would affect the team. He made sure they avoided negative influences, weren't being pulled into a gang, weren't flunking school—that they were in fact going to class—and that there wasn't any alcohol in the dorm rooms.

On the surface, it might seem that the most glamorous role is that of head coach. He's out front in public, everybody knows his name (not everyone knows the names of the assistant coaches), and during the games he is the strategic operator. But he can't do his job if the recruiter doesn't bring promising players to him. And if the scout doesn't do his job, the team won't know what to expect when they face their opponents on the floor. The coach who has the least visible role (and maybe the most thankless task) is the guy who makes sure the players are going to class and not boozing it up on weekends. But if he isn't doing his job, if players aren't keeping up academically, *you don't have a team*. The impact of that coach's role is critical.

All the coaching roles are vital. The absence of any of these roles could literally stop the team in its tracks.

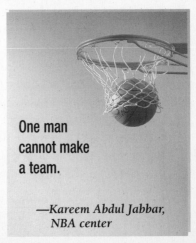

One man cannot make a team.

—*Kareem Abdul Jabbar,*
NBA center

The point is, everyone's role on a coaching staff is important. And everyone's role on the family "staff" is important as well. Dad and Mom have different roles, often with different areas of responsibility, even though some tasks may be shared. It's not my purpose here to say who should earn the major income or who should take out the trash. But I do think it's important that each family understands that every success-ful team does have a breakdown of responsibilities. Every couple needs to be clear about what those roles will be and how those roles work together in order to bring about the "end" that they desire.

The other reality is that every successful entity has a "head." Every sports team has a head coach. Every corporation has a CEO. Every

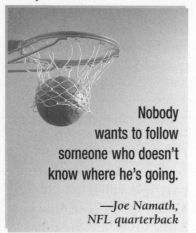

Nobody wants to follow someone who doesn't know where he's going.

—Joe Namath, NFL quarterback

school has a principal. Every family, too, needs a head. Here's where many fami-lies get bogged down.

Traditionally the head of the family has been the husband and father, except in homes where the father was not present. In that case, Mom was the family head by default, and my hat is off to my own mother and the many single moms like her who have valiant-ly shouldered the tough roles of being both father and mother, breadwinner and homemaker.

But today father-absence in our society has reached a critical point, leaving almost 30 percent of our nation's children without a father fulfilling his role in the home.[5] The impact on our children and our society is chilling: 90 percent of all runaway and home-less youths, 85 percent of all youths sitting in prisons, and 71 per-cent of all high school dropouts come from fatherless homes.[6] Does this mean that all children from fatherless homes are headed for doom? Or that kids from two-parent homes are guaranteed to turn out great? Of course not! I wouldn't be what I am today if sta-tistics ruled the day. But it doesn't do any of us any good to put our heads in the sand and ignore the fact that father-absence puts

---

[5]U.S. Bureau of the *Census, Current Population Report*, Series P23–193, March 1997. The actual figures in 1997 were: 27 percent of all children were living with only one parent (usually the mother), and 35 percent of these were living with a parent who had never been married.

[6]Figures compiled by the Alliance for Non-Custodial Parents Rights, P.O. Box 80438, Santa Barbara, CA 93118–0438.

our kids at risk and is having serious social implications.[7]

Unfortunately even some fathers *in* the home are so busy with their work and careers that managing the home and raising the kids are virtually left to Mom. Or we've simply gotten lazy and not faced our responsibilities as husbands and fathers.

A friend of mine—I'll call him Jim—used to leave managing the family finances to his wife. She was very budget conscious and accounted for all expenditures. By his own admission, Jim had a more laissez-faire approach. "I didn't run up big debts," he told me, "but my attitude was, if we had money in our pockets we could spend it—with no real planning or responsibility for my family's financial future other than bringing home my paycheck. I left stretching the money to my wife."

But one day his frustrated wife drew the line: "*You* pay the bills from now on." Jim agreed and admits it was a revelation to him. Not only did he begin to feel responsibility for his family's financial well-being but also his overall responsibility to his family as "head of the family" began to deepen. "I realized that my wife's happiness and well-being were my responsibility. If my wife or kids weren't doing well, I had to answer for it."

Jim realized his wife was overwhelmed with home and family responsibilities and had lost a lot of self-confidence about her other talents and gifts. When their youngest child was ready for preschool, he strongly encouraged his wife to brush up on her skills and get back into her field of work, gradually increasing the amount of time she put into it as the kids got older. By the time the last one left home, both Jim and his wife were successfully running their own business.

Again, my purpose is not to say who should pay the bills. But if we're comparing parenting to coaching, someone has to take the responsibility of being "head coach" or the staff and the team aren't going to function properly. The head coach needs to make it his or her business to see that everyone is working in unity for the success of the team. Someone needs to say, "The buck stops here." Without it, responsibility gets shifted back and forth and sometimes creates confusion as to who is taking responsibility for what. Who hasn't seen kids trying to play Mom against Dad to get what they want, or a spouse undermining the authority of the other? A "head coach" helps give focus and brings order to the family.

The role of "head coach" is not a position of personal privilege; it's a

---

[7]Ibid. ANCPR. (Children from fatherless homes are 5 times more likely to commit suicide, 32 times more likely to run away, 20 times more likely to have behavioral disorders, 14 times more likely to commit rape, 9 times more likely to drop out of school, 10 times more likely to abuse chemical substances, 9 times more likely to end up in a state-operated institution, 20 times more likely to end up in prison.

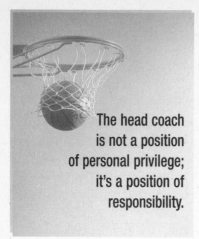

The head coach is not a position of personal privilege; it's a position of responsibility.

position of overall responsibility for the team. If a sports team has a losing streak, whom do the fans, the media, and the owner hold responsible? The head coach.

The whole discussion of roles on a coaching staff or in a family is not about who is more worthy or more valuable. It's about the important function that each role plays. The "positions" were in place before the staff was. The people *fill* the roles that have already been established. And in the family, kids need the security of *both* Dad and Mom taking responsibility for their roles.

As I mentioned before, my mom raised us kids on her own. She did a fantastic job, given the challenges of working double shifts and trying to keep us out of trouble. But is that the way it's supposed to be—moms raising their kids on their own? I don't think so. There was a void in my life—a void that was filled by a coach who took a fatherly interest in me.

The role of father has been marginalized in our society—for a complex web of reasons—and mothers have been shouldering the lion's share of the responsibility for raising the kids. I personally feel that we men need to accept overall responsibility for the well-being of our families—not as "head boss," but as "head coach."

There's a difference.

An effective head coach builds up everyone on the staff; the staff needs to feel like a team. Husband and wife need to experience a real partnership, even with different roles and responsibilities. The head coach can't be in it for himself. He's in there for the good of the whole team. If he *is* in it for himself, his position is weakened. If he's in it for the perks, if his primary goal is to further his own career, if he expects everyone to say, "How high?" when he says, "Jump," if he doesn't take the time to foster good communication, if he fails to respect the input of his staff or neglects to build up the strengths of each player, the team will begin to suffer.

A good head coach puts the team first. The best head coaches are literally servants in the background. They provide a strong foundation for the people they have been called to lead so that the players can excel. If the coach is doing his job right, the players' lives are uplifted and they get the opportunity to move forward and thrive.

Maybe you watched the Chicago Bulls win their six championships. Fantastic hoops! Phil Jackson, as everyone knows, was an important and integral part of the Bulls as head coach. He's the kind of coach that ends up in the Hall of Fame. But when people talk about the Chicago Bulls, whose names leap into the spotlight? Michael Jordan, Scottie Pippen, Toni Kukoc, Dennis Rodman, Ron Harper.

As an effective head coach, Phil Jackson helped put the people in his charge in the best positions to obtain their goals and dreams. The entire team benefited. Rarely do you see a head coach projecting himself as the person responsible for the success of the team. He's always reflecting back to the players—always.

This is how coaching works. This is how I believe the family works best too.

INSTANT REPLAY

The bottom line for strong relationships on the coaching staff is respect. Each of the topics addressed in this chapter—loyalty, communication, and role affirmation—serves the objective of respecting one another.

As a coach, I set the example and required respect for everyone connected with the team. We respected each person for what he represented as a person and as a part of our organization. We taught our players that withholding respect until someone earned it would backfire. Everyone needs to be respected first for who they are.

On the team, we taught respect for the coaches, the players, and the managers simply because each person was part of the team. In case you are wondering what a manager does, he basically keeps everything moving smoothly, sees that everyone has what he or she needs, and even cleans up the locker room.

One of the first times I got in trouble with a coach—Coach Lester, back in high school—was when he felt that I had disrespected our manager. I had purposely left my towel on the floor, enjoying the idea of a manager as my personal servant.

"He has better things to do than to pick up after you!" Coach Lester shouted. "He serves the team—just like I do—not your laziness or your ego!"

For the first time I realized that Coach Lester considered the manager to be as important as the coaches. I got the message. How we treated the coach was how we treated the manager. We needed to treat our manager with great respect. He didn't have to earn it. He didn't have to be a high scorer. He just had to be who he was, doing his part of the job, and we were expected to respect his role equally.

The best thing about this atmosphere of respect is that it frees every-body from trying to one-up the next person. You are granted respect; you don't have to prove anything. Any lack of respect reflects the char-acter of the person withholding it more than that of the person who should receive it. It is a classic application of the Golden Rule: "Do to others as you would have them do to you."[8]

The respect we have for our spouse goes way beyond the big brown eyes or sense of humor or outgoing personality we fell in love with. Respect is grounded in the fact that he or she is a person of value in God's eyes.

And it's granted for the important role this person plays as "mother of my kids" or "father in this family"—whether or not that person is the perfect spouse or perfect parent. If we have this kind of respect for each other on the family "staff," we will be creating a strong relationship for coaching our kids *together* in the game of life.

---

[8]Luke 6:31, the Holy Bible.

FREE THROW

1. Practicing loyalty

In the following situations, suggest how family loyalty can be preserved while dealing responsibly with the issue at hand.

(a) When you take your daughter to the toy store to spend her allowance, she begs to buy a Barbie doll. You know that your spouse personally disapproves of this doll because of the unrealistic feminine image it plants in your daughter's mind, but you only halfway agree.

(b) Your spouse forgets to bring the ice cream (your family's contribution) to your family's annual reunion. What should you say?

(c) You receive a phone call from your child's school informing you that your child missed three classes that morning. What should you do?

2. Communication

The following acrostic[9] includes a self-evaluation scale. Indicate with an X on each scale how well communication functions in your "coaching staff." Let one represent strong communication and five represent weak elements that need improvement.

---

[9]Adapted from Bryon Emmert, "Communication Counsel," *Husbands and Wives* (Wheaton, Ill.: Victor Books, 1988), 286.

<u>Strong</u>   <u>Weak</u>

C—Commit yourself to listening to your spouse every day.

           1   3   5

O—Observe each other's unspoken needs.

           1   3   5

M—Make regular appointments to spend time together and talk.

           1   3   5

M—Mend your arguments before you go to bed.

           1   3   5

U—Utilize the opportunities to let your actions speak louder than words.

           1   3   5

N—Notice the positive things your spouse does, and say thanks.

           1   3   5

I—Initiate conversation by asking feeling-oriented questions.

           1   3   5

C—Care about your spouse's opinions, even if they differ from yours.

           1   3   5

A—Admit to your spouse when you're wrong.

           1   3   5

T—Touch each other when you listen or talk.

           1   3   5

E—Expect the best of your spouse.

           1   3   5

3. Talking about roles

If you are married, both you and your spouse should do this exercise. Without discussing it ahead of time with your spouse, write four brief paragraphs answering the following questions.

    (a) What is your own role and responsibilities in the family at this time?

    (b) Are there ways in which you'd like your role or responsibilities to change?

    (c) What is your spouse's role and responsibilities in the family at this time?

    (d) Are there ways in which you'd like your spouse's role or responsibilities to change?

Once you have finished, discuss your responses with your spouse. Listen carefully to what he or she says, and then seek agreement on any adjustments. (Don't forget to affirm your spouse and express appreciation for positive ways that he or she carries out his or her role and responsibilities.)

3. YOUR DREAM TEAM

Man! Sherialyn and I were *rea-dy*. We had this parenting thing all geared up and rarin' to go. We'd taken Lamaze childbirth classes, we had the crib and the diapers, we'd been reading all the childcare books . . . .

Then the day arrived when the doctor said, "Congratulations! You're the father of a healthy baby girl!" and laid that beautiful, squirming little bundle in my hands. *My* hands! I held my firstborn out in front of me and looked at her little fist balled up in the air . . . and panicked. *Wait a minute! What am I supposed to do now?*

I had a similar experience the following year when the athletic director for the University of Detroit Mercy called me to announce that I'd been selected as the head coach of their basketball team.

Head coach! My own team! Man, I was ready. What I had prepared for so long had finally come to pass. I was eager to meet my players, set our goals, build relationships, and develop a winning team. The next day I hopped on the plane with my heels clicking and my dreams spinning, and that euphoria lasted all the way to Detroit and through the news conference. Finally, when I was finished grinning and answering reporters' questions, the athletic director said, "That was good. That was good. We're going to have a great year. Now, why don't you head on over to the locker room and meet your players. They're waiting for you."

Halfway there I panicked. Yeah . . . they *were* waiting for me, and I had no idea what to say to them! I turned around and literally ran back to the office and asked to use the phone. I found a secluded spot, where I wouldn't be overheard, and called Coach Lute Olson back at the University of Arizona, where I had been an assistant for six years. "Hey, Coach," I said in a muffled voice, "I'm about to meet my players. What's the first thing I should say to these guys?"

Now, I had a pretty good idea of how I wanted to relate to my team, and Coach Olson knew this. I knew that a team would play their hearts out for a coach they felt had their good in mind. But this was the day "the baby was going to be placed in my hands," and we needed an introduction. "Well, Ricky," Coach Olson growled on the other end of the line, "The first thing ya gotta do is get their attention."

Get their attention, huh? I entered the locker room—fifteen pairs of eyes watching my every move. Looking around, I noticed that several of the guys were wearing caps. With a few quick strides I snatched caps off their heads and made a big fuss about that kind of disrespectful behavior interfering with the team's success. I never saw so many wide eyes and open mouths.

Coach Olson had the right idea; I needed their attention, and I had it. They knew a new sheriff had come to Dodge!

I relaxed and grinned. "Hi. I'm Coach Byrdsong. . . ."

1. THEY'RE NOT A BOTHER

Having gotten the attention of my players, I was quick to assure them that I was excited to be their coach and that I was confident we were going to have a great year. And it was true. On that first day with the University of Detroit Mercy basketball team, I felt privileged to have fifteen of the most unique guys in the world standing in front of me. I told them so, and I kept on telling them during the whole season.

Have you ever noticed how often a coach pats his players on the backside? This is an acceptable ritual in sports for communicating esteem and affection—a form of encouragement no matter how the game is going.

As a parent, that's my first task as well. My children did not ask to come into this world or into our family (a fact they like to remind me of sometimes when they are upset and think it will shock me). Nevertheless, it was through an act of love that we conceived them, and every day they are here, one of the things I want to communicate to them is that I'm excited they are a part of our family.

I believe we need to let our kids know over and over that we feel fortunate to be their parents and to have the privilege of raising them— not only when they're cute and cuddly toddlers but when they're gawky teenagers. Not only when they're good but when they're mad or sad or acting bad. Too many of us forget as the years go by how excited we were when our kids entered the world. Back then we picked them up so often the little buggers hardly got any rest. We bounced them on our knee, threw them in the air, talked baby talk to them, and generally made utter fools of ourselves—that's how excited we were. We did all those little affectionate things when they were small, but too often as they grow older, we move away from overt expressions of our love and care. (How many adolescent boys in trouble with the law admit bitterly, "My dad never hugged me or said, 'I love you.'")

My preteen might cringe when I hug her in front of her friends, but that doesn't mean she doesn't want my expressions of love. I just need to find new ways of showing love that respect her increasing maturity. Each day is a new day, and we must stress our love for our children in new, fresh ways.

Even as a coach, I had to find new ways to communicate my enthusiasm for the team members. One way was to show interest in things that mattered to them outside of basketball. I often called various team members just to find out how they were doing. How were their classes going? How were their families doing back home? Occasionally I even took team members to church with me. Those personal expressions showed the team that their performance on the court wasn't my only interest in them. I cared about them as people and was happy when they were around.

If they wanted to talk to me, I made sure I found the time. They weren't bothering me. They were *my team*.

Likewise, in the family it is so important that our kids never think we consider them a bother. Sure, caring for them is hard work! Sometimes we get exasperated and lose our patience. But they should *always* know that their value to us far outweighs the time, the effort, and the rough spots.

How can they know that? Only if we tell them.

Some parents relate best to babies and toddlers; others (often dads) put their gears in "Park" until the kids can throw a little ball around. And too many of us throw up our hands when the kids hit those baffling teen years. But both parents—Mom and Dad—need to learn to relate to and enjoy their kids at every age.

Dads, be willing to engage in the lives of your little children by participating in the games they want to play. When my kids were younger, it seemed like they wanted to go to the park six times a day! It would have been so easy to say, "What? We just left the park." But in their world at that age, that's what was important to them. So I went to the park . . . six times a day!

Love is spelled T-I-M-E!

—Zig Ziglar, master salesperson

When kids are older, it's easy to narrow our focus down to how they're doing in school. But grades can be a sore point that shuts down conversation if that's your only concern. Sure, ask them about school—but be interested in more than their schoolwork. How are they getting along with their friends? Are there any new activities they'd like to get involved in? Better yet, how do they feel about their school, their town, the world they're growing up in? What do they think about the results of a recent election?

A great time for this exchange is at the dinner table. (I hope you have meals together. Tragically, too many families have given up this daily tradition.) You might end up learning things you'd never discover by more direct questions. And don't be put off by terse comments like, "It's OK," "Fine," "Uh, pretty good." Sometimes kids are just testing whether you really do want to know. Sometimes they simply haven't put their thoughts into words yet. Keep trying; at least you are showing them that you care. It's important that kids know that what's important to them is also important to you.

Just in case you're not convinced, think about yourself and your spouse. Isn't it important that on a regular basis your spouse lets you know that you are more than just a piece of furniture around the house? You want to be noticed; you want someone to pay attention to the things that are important to you; you want to feel that your spouse enjoys spending time with you. If your spouse is not doing this, it's easy to feel, "She [or he] just doesn't care." Don't foster the same feelings in the lives of your children.

2. THEY'RE NOT A BURDEN

A coach assures his or her players that their basic needs will be met as long as they are part of the team. They will be fed and sheltered and given medical attention, and academic support as well. In amateur sports, of course, we weren't allowed to provide other necessities, such as clothing and transportation. But as student athletes, we covered their big needs. We wanted them to know they did not have to worry about those areas of life for as long as they were part of the team. That wasn't their job; it was our job.

Children have a similar need to be free from worry about the basic necessities of life. In any family there may be times when the resources are short and we have to tell our children that we can't afford this or that. That's OK. (In fact, it's important that our children learn that they can't always get everything they want.) But there are ways to say no or wait without creating anxiety or making them feel that the family's tight financial situation is their fault.

He ain't heavy; he's my brother.

*—The Hollies,
recording artists, 1969*

Unfortunately many kids feel they are a burden to their parents. How often do they hear, "I'm tired; don't bother me. I work hard all day to put a roof over your head, isn't that enough?" or "I could take your mother to Acapulco if we didn't have to pay these outrageous orthodontist bills!" In our frustration, we may make our kids feel as though we're doing them a favor by providing their necessities—or worse, that we resent having to do so. But it is destructive to any child's self-esteem when they feel a significant adult—particularly a parent—wishes he or she didn't have such a "burden."

Do kids need to learn responsibility and to not be wasteful with the things we provide? Absolutely! But if you are struggling financially and want to talk about it with them, explain to them the facts relating to the situation. This will assure them that it's not their fault. They are children! You are the adult. Let them know that providing for them is your job, and that you are going to take care of them joyfully and to the best of your ability.

3. ARTICULATE YOUR GOALS FOR THEM

As head coach of a college team, my job was to create the best team possible. One of my first objectives was to articulate my goals for the team and sell them on the value of those goals so that they would make them their personal goals. Now, you might think that the goal is obvious: to win!—and that each team member would naturally agree. But it's not that simple. Since I really loved my players, my goals included much more than just "winning." I wanted to communicate that I had their best interests at heart.

Whenever I'd talk to a team as their coach, I'd say, "Hey, I'm here to help you accomplish your goals and aspirations. We all want to win, but in order for that to happen, there are certain things that you must be able to do." I articulated those things in what I call a "Team Mission Statement" (see appendix B). I needed to be careful what values the mission statement communicated. Did I want my team to be the highest-scoring team in America? Or did I want them to be the most efficient offensive team they could be? The goals I set for the team had a tremendous impact on what my team focused on, as well as the personality and character it developed. A team that is trying to be the high-scoring team in America may end up shooting shot after shot with very little thought, while a team focused on offensive efficiency may not seem to score as many points. But if the latter team scores on the *majority* of their shots, they can actually win more games.

In a similar way, I prepared a mission statement for my kids (see appendix A). Having such a mission statement focuses on what we want to accomplish. In both instances, my first concern was *attitude*. To me, attitude is more important than skill or talent, because attitude affects not only what we want to accomplish but also *how* we go about it. If you look at the mission statements I prepared for both the Northwestern team and for my own children, you'll notice

> Once you get a taste of where you want to go, motivation takes care of itself.
>
> —*Chuck Daly,*
> *NBA coach*

that "gratefulness" is first on the list. A grateful attitude leaves no room for selfishness or demanding that the world "owes" you something. Instead, gratefulness acknowledges that all good things are gifts from God and that we owe whatever successes or privileges we enjoy to the efforts and sacrifices of others. A person with a grateful attitude makes a good "team player."

Popular author and pastor Charles Swindoll has said, "The longer I live, the more I realize the impact of attitude on life." He continues,

> Attitude, to me, is more important than facts. It is more important than the past, than education, than money, than circumstances, than failures, than successes, than what other people think or say or do. It is more important than appearance, giftedness or skill. It will make or break a company . . . a church . . . a home. The remarkable thing is we have a choice every day regarding the attitude we will embrace for that day. We cannot change our past . . . we cannot change the fact that people will act in a certain way. We cannot change the inevitable. The only thing we can do is play on the one string we have and that is our attitude . . . I am convinced that life is 10 percent what happens to me and 90 percent how I react to it. And so it is with you . . . we are in charge of our attitudes.[1]

A mission statement should also address *why* something is important. Should we set a goal that our kids will not smoke cigarettes? Or would it be more effective to say that we want our kids to value their health? If we focus only on getting them to avoid smoking, we may or may not accomplish that particular goal. But if we try to get our kids to value their health—and succeed—we may protect them from the ravages of smoking *plus* instill in them an attitude that addresses several other health-related issues.

Have you ever thought about what you really want to accomplish with your kids? Have you ever tried to articulate the goals you have for them—or thought about how best to communicate those goals? Do you want them to get good grades, go to college, get a good job? How do those goals fit into your larger mission and purpose for your kids? What must take place for that mission to be accomplished?

---

[1]Charles R. Swindoll, *Strengthening Your Grip* (Dallas: Word, Inc., 1982).

4. DEFINE SUCCESS

In order for a coach or a parent to articulate their goals, they must first define success. Most kids come to a sports program believing "success" is how many games they win or how many points they score. But as a coach, I quickly dispelled that notion. I wanted my players to understand that those things are by-products of a greater definition of success: *continual growth toward excellence in every phase of the game* (not a bad definition of success for a family, either). For me, success also meant

(1) At the end of the journey, we would still be intact; no one would have to quit the team.

(2) We would have worked as hard as we possibly could at all times, win or lose.

(3) Honesty and integrity would be our foundation. (If we won a game but did not win fairly and by the rules, we couldn't call that victory a success.)

Once we articulate what success is for our kids, they will be watching what we applaud and what we reward. Do we get excited about the A our child gets on a school paper, even though we know he copied most of his work out of a book? Are we constantly bragging that one of our kids could be a fashion model? Do we push our kids toward "prestigious" schools or jobs even though they might have other interests? If these are not the things you said mattered most to you, your kids will notice such inconsistencies.

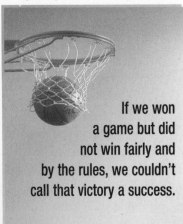

If we won a game but did not win fairly and by the rules, we couldn't call that victory a success.

Here's some ancient wisdom: Two centuries ago Jesus said, "Whoever can be trusted with very little can also be trusted with much, and whoever is dishonest with very little will also be dishonest with much."[2] At some point, the issues of honesty and integrity always surface. If we don't want to set our kids up for failure, we must base our foundation for success on honest efforts as well as honest results.

---

[2]Luke 16:10, the Holy Bible.

5. EVERYONE IS DIFFERENT—TREAT THEM THAT WAY

A sports team is a *team*—but each player is an individual and brings unique gifts and talents to the team. It was important for me as a coach not only to recognize this but also to let the players know that I saw and appreciated their uniqueness. If I tried to make everyone into point guards, no matter how good they became, the team would be ineffective without a center or forwards. Even people in the same positions develop specialties—defense, offense, rebounding. For a team to be effective, it is important that we first identify and call out the many unique gifts among us, then blend and share these gifts. When we bring all of that together, we will have a team that will function more effectively and at a higher level.

Every player on my teams came equipped not only with talent and skills but also with personality qualities. I came to value the players who were intense and emotional as well as the players who were more steady and reserved. A strong, aggressive player might be perfect as an "enforcer," someone who could hold position "in the paint," where players tend to be more physical and rough. On the other hand, an aggressive kid could get himself thrown out of the game at the very moment I needed him if I didn't coach him on how to handle his gift.

I've had low-key players on my teams that we encouraged to be more outgoing, and aggressive players that had to be toned down a bit, but we certainly did not do a major overhaul with either personality trait. We tried to get the most out of each player in line with his own strengths, and would not have wanted it to be any other way.

In the same way that, as a coach, I took the time to determine each of my player's gifts and abilities, I must determine the gifts and abilities of my children. Before my youngest, Ricky, could even tie his shoes, he was banging on tables, pounding on chairs, and beating out rhythms with spoons, sticks, whatever he could lay his hands on, until I realized what was in his soul. This kid is a drummer. Of course, we didn't want him banging on the furniture, so his mother decided to purchase a drum set for him to redirect his energy. Today, at the tender age of eight, he

People only do their best at things they truly enjoy.

—*Jack Nicklaus, golf legend*

can play a set of traps behind the band at our church like you would-n't believe, while the whole congregation sings along.

Likewise, in your family, you need to discover your kids' gifts and then direct them in constructive paths. Remember that every quality can either be *used* or *abused*. The kid who is more aggressive can use that attribute in a positive way *if* it is channeled toward taking initiative and being assertive. The child who is stubborn by nature might have the personality to be uncompromising in a just cause.

Observe and evaluate what seems to attract and motivate your children. Learn what their likes and dislikes are. Perhaps you'd like all your kids to play some kind of sport. If one child is outgoing and likes being around other people, you might guide her toward team sports. If she is more introverted but has a lot of energy, you might involve her in something like tennis. The benefits of discipline and physical activity might be similar, but expressed in different ways. Think about these motivations for each area of your child's life.

I sometimes hear older parents express disappointment in how different their offspring have turned out. In bewilderment they say, "I raised them both the same. How could they turn out so different?" But this is to be expected. Kids really *are* different. What works with one won't necessarily work with another.

In *The New Birth Order Book*,[2] Dr. Kevin Leman identifies many character traits that result simply from whether a child is firstborn, middle-born, last-born, the only child, or the only child of one gender. One implication of his research is that you *can't* treat your children the same because each one's position in the family profoundly affects how he or she will experience your treatment. Another of his claims is that you naturally and rightly modify your parenting with experience. But more importantly, *who* each child is deserves individualized treatment. Some children are devastated by "the look"; others have to be spoken to firmly at least three times before you can get their attention. Rewards and punishments may work with one; reasoning may work with another. One may be naturally independent and not seem to need much attention. Another may be lost and devastated if you are not right there all the time.

Failure to realize that you need to treat your children differently can have the effect of trying to fit a square peg into a round hole. This does

[2]Kevin Leman, *The New Birth Order Book* (Grand Rapids, Mich: Fleming H. Revell Co., 1998).

not mean that you teach different values to your children or treat them unfairly. There should be no unfairness or favoritism, but what your firstborn needs at age twelve may be different from what your youngest needs at that same age.

It is important that we as parents don't label one of our kids as being "better" or "easier" than another. We must understand that each of our kids is special and unique and that his or her uniqueness is a strength. We need to encourage our kids with whatever personality traits they have, because there is a place for every quality. Sure, every kid needs to be "polished" in some way or another, but don't squelch the gift, channel it!

6. REALISTIC EXPECTATIONS

Early in my coaching career, I called a more experienced coach and complained about some of my players who were about to flunk and didn't seem to care. I told him I'd done everything possible to help them but they'd just shrugged it off. To my surprise, my friend seemed less concerned about the kids' behavior than about my response. "You should have known this would happen with some of your new players," he said. "It happens every year about this time. You've gotta take it in stride."

It turned out I wasn't alone. Many new coaches become frustrated over the surprises they face in coaching young players. Kids will let you down in so many different ways—missing classes, not paying their bills on time, doing the very thing you told them not to do. Furthermore, this is the first time most of them have been away from home, and Mama and Papa are not around to cover for them. A coach who does not realize that this behavior comes with the territory is likely to become so frustrated that he or she starts labeling the kids as impossible and communicates a dislike for them.

My friend's response changed my perspective on coaching. Never again did I let my disappointment over a player's behavior frustrate me to the point that I didn't want to be bothered with him. In fact, as the years went by, I

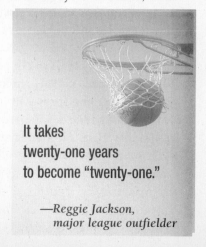

It takes twenty-one years to become "twenty-one."

—*Reggie Jackson,*
major league outfielder

began to anticipate that certain problems would surface with a number of kids. Developing more realism in my expectations didn't mean I became more tolerant of misbehavior. It was my job to deal with misbehavior, but I wasn't so blown away by it that I wanted to give up on my players. And that realism gave me the equilibrium to respond firmly but constructively.

The same thing needs to happen in our role as parents. *Kids will be kids, yes, but parents must continue to be parents* and not bail out just because their unrealistic expectations aren't met. Unrealistic expectations often lead to frustration, frustration develops into anger, and anger produces resentment and disgust with the kids and the whole parenting process.

Friends of mine who are new grandparents sometimes joke that if they had known grandparenting would be so great, they would have done it first! One of the things that makes being a grandparent easier is perspective on what to expect and the ability to see many "crises" as predictable, manageable, even normal. If a four-year-old breaks the antique lamp that's been in your family for three generations, it's tempting to scream, "How could you?" and go ballistic. But that's the type of thing young kids do. They're not completely coordinated, they don't understand how delicate an old lamp is, and they don't comprehend its value to you. Understanding all this (a perspective granted most grandparents) helps you to avoid an attitude of anger and resentment toward the child. In fact, having realistic expectations may help you to anticipate accident potential and, in this case, put the lamp out of reach.

If you follow sports, you'll notice that coaches talk about wanting veteran teams, because veteran teams are the teams that win. The reason for this is that younger teams are prone to make more mistakes due to the simple fact that they have not had the opportunity to understand the game in its fullest context. Parents of young children need to remember this too. Each child is inexperienced in the phase of life he or she is entering. They will make mistakes. Your job is to guide them safely through it.

I know there is a good chance that one day my son or my daughters will come home smelling like cigarette smoke, beer, or something stronger. I don't want that to happen, and I am doing everything I can to prevent it, but I'm prepared if it does. *Knowing* that kids may experiment or push the limits is not the same as condoning something. Instead of being so shocked that such a thing could happen that I become frozen with grief or outraged with disappointment, I want to be ready to respond wisely. How I respond at that moment will have a whole lot to do with whether their foolish experiment develops into a pattern of rebellion, addiction, and destruction or whether it becomes an opportunity for instruction and correction.

7. DON'T BE A FOOL

Not going nuts if your kid tries marijuana is not the same as being so naïve that you can't detect its smell or recognize the trappings of at-risk behavior and druggie friends. Don't be a fool; you have to be alert and set up appropriate safeguards.

Several years ago the national news carried a story that took place in Chicago, my "backyard." Two teenage brothers were arrested for the murder of an eleven-year-old. After the trial, a friend of mine had a chance to talk to the boys' mother. Ernestine was a public school-teacher, and she and her husband tried to provide a good home for their three children. Her daughter did well in school, graduated from college, and even went on to work on her master's degree.

Her two teenage sons, Derrick and Cragg, seemed to be doing OK too. But there were some things, she said, that should have made her suspicious. One day Cragg came home driving a car that belonged to "a friend," but Ernestine didn't insist on knowing *which* friend or even whether Cragg had a valid driver's license. The boys always seemed to have money and said it came from doing yard work in the neighbor-hood, but she never checked out *whose* yard.

The family lived in a nice neighborhood with good schools. Ernestine wanted to believe the best about her sons, so she didn't ques-tion their appearance, lifestyle, friends, or attitudes. After all, they were always polite and loving toward her, and they were still so young— Derrick was fourteen and Cragg was sixteen.

Then on September 1, 1994, the Hardaway brothers were arrested for the gangland-style murder of eleven-year-old Robert "Yummy" Sandifer, who had been wanted by police for a shooting spree a few days earlier. As it turned out, all three boys were members of one of Chicago's notorious street gangs. Derrick is now serving forty-five years in prison; Cragg is serving sixty.

Wiser now, Mrs. Hardaway passes on the lesson she learned too late: "Parents, be alert to things that just don't fit, that don't make sense— and then follow through."

She's right. As a coach, one of the things I tried to do was get to know my team members' friends. I knew that the more time I spent around my players and the things they enjoyed doing, the better chance I had to make them aware of certain dangers. I didn't just rush in at the last moment blowing whistles; I was there the whole time.

I figure that's the best way I can help prevent my children from making wrong choices too. I need to know their friends, know the pressures and temptations they face, and how to recognize the danger signals. But being involved with our kids and their friends doesn't mean we have to dress in the latest outrageous fashion or talk street talk with them. They know we're "ancient," so we better act our age. But even the hippest dude or coolest chick can recognize someone who's genuinely interested in him or her.

(Here's a tip: If you're having trouble connecting with your kids' friends, you can always fall back on food. Few kids can resist it, even when it's served at your house!)

8. COUNT TO TEN

Since "kids will be kids," it doesn't take much for us to be frustrated or disappointed in them. But what happens next is often critical to whether molehills become mountains or we recognize this as just a bump in the road.

Whenever I was disappointed with my team's behavior or performance on the court, I learned to step back from the situation and tell the players that I would talk to them later about it. Many coaches have learned to follow this general rule. They may make general comments expressing their disappointment at the time, but they do not get into discussing the game per se until later.

There are several reasons for this policy. *First*, when emotions are running high, they tend to cloud our thinking. We are likely to say something that will have a negative impact on a player and even cause severe hurt. *Second*, once we step back from a situation, we have the chance to make a more informed analysis. In the heat of disappointment it may appear that the fault rests with one person, when less emotional scrutiny may reveal a more complex cause. We don't want to blame something on someone where blame is not appropriate. *Third*, we might discover that we did not prepare our team as well as we should have. Others are far more receptive to correction when they see us accepting our share of the responsibility. (Usually they've already identified our responsibility anyway, so there's no advantage in trying to conceal it.)

This approach also applies when we're "coaching" our kids. When our children disappoint us, regardless of the situation, the moment we realize that we're going to react out of anger, shock, or frustration, we should simply express our disappointment and agree to discuss it later. This gives us time to reflect on the issues: What is the real problem? Is it possible that we're making more of it than we should? Was it a legitimate accident that is unlikely to occur again? If not, is there something going on behind the scenes that caused the problem?

Also, before you leap in to "fix" something, give your kids an opportunity for some input. Try to understand the situation from his or her point of view. It also helps to be compassionate and seek to understand the pressures your child is under. This less threatening approach may also give you a chance to find out whether your kid has exhibited this particular behavior before in another setting.

This doesn't mean going soft or not dealing with the problem. It only means that you are interested in identifying the real source of the problem so that it can be effectively addressed. But if you overreact and don't give your child an opportunity to express what's really going on, you may drive him or her to the very people who created the negative peer pressure in the first place and expose your child to more problems.

If you can help your child deal with the pressures that led to the problem, you may discover that he or she is no longer interested in participating in such behavior. If this is the case, they'll see you as a helper, a friend, a true coach.

9. PRESERVE THE RELATIONSHIP

If you talk to the world's greatest coaches, they will tell you that in every game someone will violate some basic principle. But the bottom line is that the game goes on, and a good coach remains calm so that he or she can think about what must be done next to lead the team forward to success. If the coach gets so angry that he or she damages relationships, the team will suffer and the game may be lost.

Expecting the unexpected became a requirement if I was to retain my role as a coach . . . and pretty much sums up my role as a parent as well. We will all have kids who make wrong choices. But if we rant and rave and say, "I can't believe you would do a thing like that!" the only response we will get—whether our kids say it to our face or not—is

"Then you don't know me, 'cause I just did it." That's not a defense of their mistake but a comment on your relationship. So believe it!

One couple went on a business trip leaving their teenage daughter in a grandmother's care. But during a phone call home, they discovered that their daughter had been spending time over at her boyfriend's house when his parents weren't home. This was a serious breach of their rules, so they canceled their remaining appointments and drove a thousand miles home to deal with the situation. Upset and disappointed, they intended to cut off the boyfriend entirely and "ground her for the rest of her natural life!" But their college son advised, "Whatever you do, don't risk destroying your relationship with her."

The parents listened. They realized that they had disapproved of the

Better bend than break.

—*Scottish proverb*

relationship from the beginning and had not been welcoming to the boy. If they cut him off entirely, would the chances be greater that their daughter would increase her sneaky behavior in order to see him? Maybe instead of holding the boyfriend at arm's length, they should get to know him and bring the relationship into their sphere of influence. So they said that if their daughter wanted to see the boyfriend, it had to be at their house when they were home. They even invited him for dinner. This was some-

thing their daughter could accept. It preserved their relationship with her. They kept talking, and before long, she broke up with the boyfriend on her own with no hard feelings toward her parents.

The game of life is a long game. You can't overreact to crises along the way or you risk alienating your kids and losing the game. Be willing to talk. Explain to your kids the dangers of their foolish behaviors. Ask probing questions as to why they did what they did and how it is likely to affect them in the long run. If you discover that a long-range view of the game seems irrelevant to them, see if you can discover why this is true. Maybe you have not been taking the long view either.

INSTANT REPLAY

I have been learning the game of golf. Each hole around the course (and the course as a whole) is labeled with a "par," the number of strokes it should take a competent player to get the ball from the tee into the cup. A par four means you should have to hit the ball only four times to get it in the hole. This way, as you go around the course, you know whether you are falling behind or playing better than what is expected.

In everyday life, we've adopted the phrase "That's par for the course" as a way to encourage someone that something is normal or to be expected. And once you look at something in this way, you can begin to focus your efforts in a more strategic manner.

But for a new player, hearing that something is "par for the course" is not always encouraging. In golf, it often took me fifteen or sixteen strokes in the beginning to get the ball into a cup that should have required only four strokes. Hearing what "par" was usually made me upset. "If this is a par four, I'll never make it!" Unfortunately my frustration never changed what par was. I finally realized I needed to focus on one thing: improving *my* swing. If I could do the next hole in fourteen strokes instead of fifteen, that would be an improvement and a source of encouragement.

The same is true in parenting. If we remain upset at the mistakes that happen along the way, we'll have no energy to focus on improvements. Good coaches understand that no matter how much they practice and teach, there will be mistakes in the game, and they must develop the ability to move on and keep looking forward. If we parents recognize the importance of keeping the relationship intact with our "players," we'll develop a "dream team" that will finish the game together.

FREE THROW

1. What is success?

There are many worthwhile goals in life. Prioritizing them can help us to focus our efforts. If your child were to ask you, "What things are most important for me to pursue in life?" how would you answer? In the list below, place an A, B, or C next to each item according to the importance you think it should have, making A most important and C least important. Add any additional goals at the end of the list.

When you have finished prioritizing, select three goals to which you have assigned an A and write a short strategy for how you might teach their importance to your children.

____ Compassion toward others
____ Education
____ Faithfulness to commitments
____ A fully funded retirement plan
____ Good health
____ Growing in excellence throughout life
____ Happiness
____ A life focused on serving others
____ Honesty and integrity in all things
____ Maintaining extended-family relationships
____ Having many friends
____ Having no consumer debt
____ Owning a home
____ Relationship with God
____ A solid marriage
____ A steady job

____ _____
____ _____
____ _____

2. Study your children

For each of your children, write a description of his or her uniqueness. Try to cover each of the following areas:

- Interests
- Skills
- The most effective long-range discipline
- The most effective short-range discipline
- What is most discouraging for this child
- What is most inspiring for this child
- What fears this child has
- How easily and quickly this child makes friends
- The most important quality in a friend to this child
- The method by which this child learns best: reading, hearing, seeing, doing . . . .
- How this child deals with change
- How this child deals with routine responsibilities
- How this child responds to peer pressure

3. Looking at your relationships with your children

(a) On a scale from 0 to 10, with 0 meaning nonexistent and 10 meaning solid, how would you rate your relationship with each of your children?

(b) No matter how good your scores are, what could you do to improve your relationship with each child if that were your sole priority in life? Write a one-paragraph statement for each child.

(c) Why not make these your priorities? There may be valid reasons why you can't make one child's needs your sole priority, but how far could you go in improving the relationship?

4. SKILLS AND DRILLS

"Hey, man, I don't know how you did it, but getting two tickets to this game ranks right up there with puttin' the first man on the moon!"

"Yeah, yeah, and what about these seats! Front row, center! Whoo-hoo!"

"Man, we're goin' to see some slam-dunkin' tonight! Heard some of the new rookies have real hot talent."

"Yeah, and this coach—the plays he pulls out of his hip pocket will knock your socks off."

"Should be a tight game. Both teams want to win badly. That'll push the score right up there."

"OK, OK, this is it. There's the whistle."

"Wait a minute. Don't those guys know they can't travel with the ball?"

"And look at that! Talk about sloppy passing. The other team's taking it away every time!"

"Uh-oh. That player's really got a temper. He's their top scorer, too. Doesn't he know those tantrums are going to get him thrown out of the game?"

"Whatsamatter here? These clowns don't even know how to dribble! How are they supposed to score if they can't even handle the ball?"

Good questions!

Most fans go to a game hoping to see some great hoops and a score that puts their team over the top. They don't think much about the hours spent on "skills and drills." The fans just want to see results!

But if the coach hasn't spent plenty of time on *fundamentals*, the team isn't going to get a chance to score, much less win the game.

As a coach, I spent a lot of time developing a game plan. Then we devised a strategy to carry it out. But both the game plan and the strategies were built on something else: the fundamentals. The fundamentals were absolutely necessary to accomplish our goal.

When I talk about fundamentals, I'm talking about *essentials*. Winning cannot happen without fundamentals. Sure, we want to score baskets—but that's not a fundamental. Fundamentals are the nitty-gritties that need to be in place in order for that basket to be scored.

In basketball, the ability to handle the ball, dribbling, and passing are fundamental to the success of scoring. So are teamwork, playing by the rules, and self-control. *A fundamental is not an end in itself but a means to an end. You will not achieve your goals without the fundamentals.*

The same is true in parenting. The game plan may be different for different families. The strategies may be different depending on the natures and personalities of the children. But it's important to teach all of our children the fundamentals—those things that are essential to any game plan if our children are going to win in the game of life.

1. EXPECT OBEDIENCE

Are your children coachable?

The number one fundamental to success in any endeavor is one that no one likes—not even adults. Call it an independent spirit, call it stubbornness, call it pride, but all of us tend to balk at "submitting" to the person in charge. Plain and simple, I'm talking about obedience.

Obedience or submission to authority is absolutely necessary to success in life.

In basketball, when my job was recruiting, the first question I asked about a would-be player was, "Is he coachable?" Every basketball coach looks for this fundamental quality in order to have a successful team. On a basketball floor, obedience is more important than skill, more important than determination, more important than courage, because obedience is what allows a player to use those gifts and abilities in their proper contexts.

Can you think of any endeavor where obedience isn't required for success to happen? Most jobs, from those in huge corporations to flipping burgers at the local malt shop, have rules and regulations that employees must obey in order for the business to run smoothly. Our whole social structure is based on a system of laws that we as citizens must obey. So it's important for me as a parent to teach my children that learning obedience is crucial to success in life.

Look at the spectator comments that opened this chapter. What would happen if the players on the team didn't follow the coach's instructions? Can you imagine the chaos and confusion on the floor? Chants would begin to rock the stadium, *"Fire the coach! Fire the coach!"* In athletics, the coach is held responsible for whether or not the team members submit to his or her authority. If the players are defiant and won't follow directions, it's the coach who has lost control of the team and he should be replaced.

Obviously parents can't be fired or replaced, but we all must hold ourselves accountable for teaching our kids this critical fundamental.

Explain the rules. As a coach, one of the first things that my staff and I did was to quickly gather the players together and explain the rules. We made it clear what was expected of them.

It's no less important for our kids to know what's expected of them. And we need to be specific. "Be home early" won't cut it. You might mean ten o'clock; your teenager is probably thinking twelve. "Clean your room!" Little Jerry probably thinks "clean" means putting the "stuff" out of sight—under the bed.

Make sure the rules are realistic. If parents expect obedience, they must also be sure the rules, and their expectations, are realistic.

A few years ago I made a rule that my players must be on time for basketball practice, but I noticed that for several days some of my players were arriving late. So I dished out discipline . . . and they were still late. It occurred to me that maybe my expectation was not realistic. So I called in the players and found out that most of them got out of class at 2:50, and I was expecting them to be in the gym at 3:00—which would have been possible only if the teacher let class out *exactly* on time and if the players sprinted all the way! The problem was solved when I changed practice time to 3:30.

At one time or another, most parents have expectations that are unrealistic. I see parents in the early stages of parenting totally frustrated because they're expecting two- and three-year-olds not to drop a glass or to sit still for long periods. This may be realistic for a ten-year-old, but probably not for your toddler. It's important to educate ourselves regarding what is appropriate behavior for different ages and stages, and to evaluate our expectations to see if they are realistic for that phase in our kid's life.

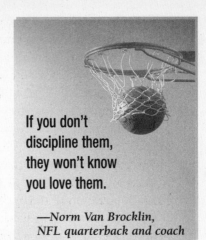

If you don't discipline them, they won't know you love them.

—Norm Van Brocklin, NFL quarterback and coach

Sherialyn and I used to dress our kids for school or church before breakfast. I mean, it made sense to *us*. You get up, you get dressed, you eat breakfast. But first thing you know, someone had spilled milk on the shirt or syrup on the dress, and we ended up frustrated. Then the kids would get upset because we made them change their clothes. This happened enough times, however, that we finally realized their level of coordination couldn't ensure that they wouldn't spill anything on their clothes. To avoid more breakfast battles on the way to our goal, we let them dress in an old T-shirt to come down to breakfast. Then after breakfast they could dress in their good clothes.

There's an old ditty that goes:

 Blessed is the man who takes his daily rub.
 Twice blest is he who washes out the tub!

I figured my kids should be "twice blest," so I asked them to clean the tub after they took their baths. But when I checked on young Ricky, the tub wasn't clean. I told him to try again. But when I checked on him a second time, it still wasn't clean. "Show me what you're doing," I said. And then I realized . . . his arms were too short! He couldn't reach all the places he needed to reach. So we decided he could clean the tub while he was still *in* the tub instead of after he got out, and while there was still a bit of water in the tub to help him begin the cleaning process.

When we discover that our expectations aren't being met, we should ask ourselves if our expectations are unrealistic.

Apply appropriate consequences. When our kids violate what is a reasonable expectation, we must apply an appropriate consequence. If we fail to implement an appropriate consequence for their disobedience or misbehavior, we are not raising our kids to respect authority;

we are not raising obedient children.

What is an appropriate consequence? A consequence should be tied as closely as possible to the *nature* of the misbehavior. Junior forgets to put away his bike? The bike is put away for a week, and he can't ride it. Princess doesn't come home on time for supper? (She's wearing a watch.) Supper is over, and there's nothing to eat till breakfast. Of course, the age of the child and understanding of the offense should be taken into consideration.

Sometimes "appropriate consequences" may be tied to the concept of *responsibility* and *privilege*. Certain *responsibilities* are appropriate to each age level—the number of household chores, care for younger siblings, lessons and homework, etc. Along with those responsibilities come certain *privileges*—allowances, amount of playtime or TV time, keys to the car. As long as your child handles his or her responsibilities, he or she can enjoy the privileges. The more responsibilities the child is given as he or she grows up, the more privileges. On the other hand, if the child is irresponsible in a certain area, it's appropriate to withdraw one or more of the privileges.

Follow through. Be consistent. One of my rules as a coach was that if a player missed a class, he did not play in the next game. What if I had an athlete who skipped class, but I let him play in the game anyway? Maybe it was an important game; maybe he was a key player. But what would I have taught the young man? That he can disobey the rules and still "play the game"—but I wouldn't have done him any favors, because you and I both know that life doesn't work that way.

As parents, we may have rules. We might even tell our kids ahead of

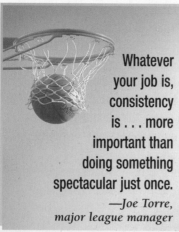

Whatever your job is, consistency is . . . more important than doing something spectacular just once.
—*Joe Torre, major league manager*

time what the consequences will be if they disobey the rules. But if we don't follow through in a consistent manner, we're teaching our kids that the rules don't really matter, that they can get away with ignoring the rules until Mom or Dad finally get fed up. Unfortunately sometimes we're just too tired to follow through (see chapter 1), or we're too distracted and busy with other things, or we don't want to cause a scene. So we give up, roll our eyes, and complain to the neighbor, "I just can't do anything with Johnny."

Oh yes, you can. Start while they're young. If you haven't started, start now.

Help them learn the correct way. After we have consistently applied appropriate consequences for disobedience, we owe it to our kids to do a fourth thing: help them learn the correct way. We may need to give them further instructions or explain the reasons behind our expectations and give them some different ways of meeting our objective so that they can do the things they enjoy. They might need help with making better decisions in order to get things done and how to sort those things out.

We also need to help our kids understand that a cooperative spirit and an obedient attitude to adults who have responsibility for them (parents, teachers, coaches) are beneficial to their well-being. The Bible says that children are to obey their parents *so that their life will be long and fruitful*.[1] The Bible calls this "the first commandment with a promise." This doesn't mean that parents have permission to be tyrants. In fact, this same Scripture passage tells fathers [parents] not to exasperate their children [be unreasonable or cruel].

But failure to teach and train our children is also a form of abuse. Not long ago two angry, violent high school students in Littleton, Colorado, killed twelve of their classmates, one teacher, and then themselves. In the wake of the massacre, the Rev. Franklin Rogers, pastor of the Fullness of Joy Church in Jonesboro, Arkansas (where a similar massacre took place by a young, violent offender), said, "A lack of discipline is child abuse. When you let children do whatever they want, that's child abuse."[2]

That's heavy-duty—but he's right. The Bible says, "If you refuse to discipline your children, it proves you don't love them; if you love your children, you will be prompt to discipline them."[3] Many people have rejected that advice because old translations use the word "rod," as in the derived adage "Spare the rod and spoil the child." But in the cases of children who have become violent, harming themselves and others, it appears their parents have spoiled—literally abused and ruined— their children by withholding discipline.

---

[1]*See Ephesians 6:1-3, the Holy Bible.*
[2]*Nightline, ABC, April 22, 1999.*
[3]*Proverbs 13:24, the Holy Bible.*

2. DEVELOP HEALTHY SELF-ESTEEM

The second fundamental critical to success in the game of life is a healthy self-esteem. At the start of every season and at the start of every game, a coach gathers his players together and encourages them. We tell them they are capable of accomplishing the goals we have set before them. I'm not talking about falsely building up egos with empty flattery, but every player is valuable to the team, and we make sure that each player knows we value him and his contribution. Some will be tremendous scorers; others will be great rebounders; still others provide a stiff defense. We don't praise scorers more than rebounders. The team will work together best when each player knows he or she is a valued member of the team and that the coaches believe he or she can do the job.

What is healthy self-esteem? A healthy self-esteem has three components: a sense of *belonging* (you are accepted), a sense of *worth* (you are valued), and a sense of *competence* (you are capable). These

Whether you think you can or you can't, you're probably right.

—*Anonymous, offered by Arnold Palmer, golf legend*

three factors are like the legs on a three-legged stool. It takes all three legs to provide a solid base for the stool. Each child should be accepted and loved for who he or she is, and we must esteem each of our children for their own unique value. As parents, we need to be careful not to praise one child's ability over another's ability. There are different kinds of ability; one is not better than another. Parents need to believe in their child and help him or her believe in their own worth and abilities.

Where does self-esteem come from? Kids feel about themselves the way the most important people in their lives feel about them. First on this list of "most important people" are parents, then teachers and coaches. In my role as coach, if I said to one of my players, "You're no good" or "You're nothing" or "You're never going to amount to anything," it would have more impact on his self-esteem than if the school bus driver said the same thing. If a child's classmates or peers make cutting remarks, that hurts—but the ultimate impact of such remarks depends on whether the people who are *most* important in his life also cut him down or whether they hold him in high regard.

This is critical. As a parent, *you* are the most important person in your child's life. So much of how your child feels about herself and about the world around her will be in relationship to the things she has heard you say or seen you do.

Who should they listen to? Even though young people will basically feel about themselves the way the most important people in their lives feel about them, that doesn't mean they can't become distracted or bent out of shape by other loud voices.

Good coaches know this. Bad press or booing fans can throw off a player's self-confidence. So I always made sure I talked to my team about whom they should listen to. I reminded them that I knew them better than the media or the fans. One mistake or a bad game wasn't the sum total of their abilities. It was important for them to pay more attention to what I was saying about them than what the media or the fans had to say.

As parents, we too must train our kids to listen to certain voices. Who really has their best self-interest at heart? The "popular" kids at school (or maybe the gangbangers) they are trying so hard to emulate? The media that dictates what's "in" or "out" or what's "hot" and what's "not"? Classmates who accept them or reject them based on what group they fit into or what table they sit at in the cafeteria? Or is it their parents, teachers, youth pastors, coaches, and loyal friends who care about them as a *person*?

No one can change his or her value. When I go to schools and speak to kids about "winning in the game of life," I often use the following illustration:

OK, so you've saved your allowance for umpteen weeks, and you've finally got $75 to buy a pair of Nike shoes. You walk in the door of the shoe store with those shoes already tap-dancing in your head. But that's when you notice that the price tag of the shoes you want reads $100. One hundred dollars! *Now* what are you going to do? So you start screaming about how ugly the shoe is, how you hate the color, and you don't like the material the shoe is made of! Now, if you were to start screaming that the shoes aren't *worth* $100, what are the chances that the store owner will lower the price of the shoe?

At this point most of the kids yell, "No way!" After they've finished demeaning the shoe, the price is still $100. The only person who can lower the price or the value of the shoe is the store owner, because he owns the shoe. A customer's opinion doesn't make any difference.

The same is true with our kids as it relates to their self-esteem. As a parent, I must make my children aware that people may put them down or say things that are demeaning, but that doesn't affect who they *really* are. God knows who they are and I know who they are.

I want my kids to understand that the only person who can lower their value is they themselves. That's why it is so important that we parents reinforce healthy images of our kids to them so that when they do encounter people who say mean and ugly things, their value in their own minds will remain intact.

Why is self-esteem so important? Because kids who consider themselves valuable tend to protect their value. Isn't that how it works with our possessions? If the weatherman predicts hail, am I going to leave my new car out in the street or put it in the garage? If you have a beautiful jade necklace that was passed down from your grandmother, are you going to wear it to the beach where it might get lost or stolen? Do you keep your money under the mattress or in the bank?

The same is true with our kids. If they value themselves highly, they will take good care of themselves. A healthy self-esteem will impact the kinds of choices they make—the kinds of friends they choose, the decision to leave harmful substances alone and not take them into their bodies, the importance of living in a way that will impact the future and eternity and not just the moment.

So, parents, don't take for granted that your kids know you love them or that they know you think they're wonderful. Tell them, "I love you," "I like your hair," "I can't imagine our family without you," "That smile makes my day!"—and tell them often. Point out your excitement and pleasure over the good things they do. It's so easy for us as parents to be negative. I recall one of my girls bringing home her report card with four A's and one C. The first thing I said was, "What happened in math?" (the C), rather than stating how pleased I was with the four A's. We need to take care that our speech builds our kids up rather than tears them down.

Even when they blow it, we should try to communicate that mistakes and failures are the result of choices they make and have nothing to do with "who they are." When kids discover they can make a different choice and get different results, they will focus more on the choices than on thinking they're just "dumb" or "uncoordinated"—all those labels that undermine their self-esteem.

There's no magic formula to promote healthy self-esteem in our kids. It simply comes down to consistently reminding them that they are special. Sometimes, before our kids head out the door to school, I will tell them to place priority on what their parents and God think of them. God has already declared them "fearfully and wonderfully made" (Psalm 139:14).

3. TEACH RESPONSIBILITY

The third fundamental for success is personal responsibility. One of the challenges of every coach is to try to get players to understand that they are personally responsible for their behavior. Our coaching staff emphasized again and again that while we may not be responsible for the things that happen to us, we are always responsible for our responses. Sometimes a player would complain that the reason he didn't get the grade he "should have gotten" in a class was because the professor didn't like him. When I followed this up with the teacher, I often discovered that there had been several violations of class procedure, which resulted in the lower grade. It was important for my players to understand this and to take responsibility for their role in the consequences they faced.

Unfortunately we are living in a culture in which no one wants to take personal responsibility. When bad things happen or when things aren't going the way we want them to, we point the finger at all sorts of reasons outside of ourselves. Black people complain that white folks are the problem; white people complain about blacks getting preferences. Women blame men; men blame women. Adult children blame their parents. Everyone's a victim!

Just the other day a twenty-something young woman who can throw a screaming fit worthy of a preschooler was blaming her husband: "He *knows* I have a hot temper, so why does he keep doing things that make me so angry?"

> Liberty trains for liberty. Responsibility is the first stem in responsibility.
>
> —W. E. B. DuBois, *African-American intellectual*

You hear that all the time among kids: "He started it"; "She made me do it"; "It's not my fault."

One way parents promote this type of thinking is by blaming their kids' misbehavior on the crowd they run with. When kids get in to trouble, I often hear their moms and dads say, "They're good kids; they're just hanging with the wrong crowd." That may be true, but that doesn't mean someone else is responsible for the rock they threw at a window or that they were caught shoplifting. Those were conscious choices made by the individual regardless of influences around him.

If we aren't teaching our kids to take personal responsibility for their own attitudes, choices, and actions, we are partly to blame.

Recently I instructed my daughter Sabrina to redo a homework assignment. Did she want to do it over? No way! Frustrated and angry, she complained to her mother (the "divide and conquer" technique). Concerned because our daughter was so upset, my wife asked me why I was making Sabrina do her paper over. I pointed out that *I* wasn't the one "making her" redo it. Sabrina was making it happen because she chose to not do it correctly the first time.

When my kids are disobedient, there are usually consequences: I'll ground them, or make them go to their room, or restrict their TV watching. I'll hear them grumbling, "Dad won't let me watch my favorite show." But I remind them that it's not "Dad's fault" they're not watching their show. When they chose to disobey *they* were choosing not to watch their show.

There's an interesting verse in the Bible that says, "But remember that the temptations that come into your life are no different from what others experience. And God is faithful. He will keep the temptation from becoming so strong that you can't stand up against it. When you are tempted, he will show you a way out so that you will not give in to it."[4] Broken down, this verse expresses three principles that we'd do well to emphasize to our children:

- Your situation is not so unusual, so don't excuse your behavior with that myth.
- Hard as your situation may be, it's not too hard for you . . . and God.
- There'll always be an opportunity to do the right thing. Look for it, *and take it!*

The truth of these principles—if we really believe them ourselves—will help our children accept the responsibility they'll need to win in the game of life. We must help them get beyond excuses such as, "He plays favorites," "It wasn't fair," "She hurt my feelings," "That teacher is

---

[4]*1 Corinthians 10:13, the Holy Bible.*

so boring." All of those things may be true, but they aren't an acceptable explanation for getting an F in a math class. A potential future employer will not care that the teacher was boring. Our kids must understand that *they* are responsible to wring from every situation what is necessary for them to succeed. And it's our job as parents to help them acquire that understanding.

What are some of the ways we can do this?

Give choices that teach responsibility. Your home should be an environment in which kids are allowed to make choices and experience the results (consequences) of their choices. Don't always make the "right choice" for them. Give them various options and later help them analyze the choices they have made.

Suppose little Hilary comes running in after school. "Mom, may I go outside to play?" Rather than just yes or no, Mom might say, "If you think you can play outside and still get your homework done by seven, when it's time for choir practice, then you may go outside and play. The choice is yours."

Now, let's say that Hilary chooses to go outside and play but does not get the homework done on time. Mom matter-of-factly tells her she must finish the homework even though it means she can't go to choir practice. What's important here is that Hilary understands that

> A man can make mistakes, but he isn't a failure until he starts blaming someone else.
> —*Sam Rutigliano,*
> *NFL and college coach*

she miscalculated and not to blame her mom for "not letting her" go to choir practice.

Unfortunately what usually happens is that a parent will get upset that the homework isn't finished, tell her child how irresponsible she is, but go ahead and let the child go to choir practice. Then the child has to stay up late to finish the homework, which makes Mom even more upset. But the parent, in shielding the child from the results of her own choices, has exacerbated the problem. You might be disappointed with how things turn out, but it's important to give your kids the opportunity to make choices for themselves and let them experience the consequences without a lot of extra dumping from you. After all, they were given a *choice*.

About a year ago my son, Ricky, got excited about joining the Cub

Scouts. But as I looked at his schedule, I didn't see how he could do it. He played hockey and basketball, he was taking drum lessons, he was in the children's choir at church, and he was a student. How could he add a full Cub Scout program? But rather than my saying no and having him be frustrated with me, I gave him a choice. I said, "Ricky, you're already involved in several different things, and I think Cub Scouts would probably crowd your schedule. But you make the choice. If you join Cub Scouts, you'll need to remain with them for at least two months. You can't go just once or twice and quit."

Even though I recommended that he not join, Ricky decided that he wanted to be a Cub Scout. Sure enough, two weeks after he joined he lost interest because there were already so many things going on in his life. However, as per our agreement, he had to keep going for two months. At the end of the two months he was able to drop out. For those two months he was frustrated, but he couldn't be frustrated with *me* because he knew up front what the choices were. He made the choice with the parameters laid out, and he knew that he was responsible for the choice he made.

Affirm kids for taking positive responsibility. Look for opportunities to affirm the results of good decision-making as well. If your son or daughter comes home and says, "Mom! Dad! I made the basketball team!" help them discover the positive steps they took toward realizing their goal.

"That's great! Why do you think you made the team?"

"Because I worked hard all summer on my game."

"You sure did! But didn't I hear you tell someone on the phone that you were so nervous you were afraid you wouldn't do well?"

"Yeah, but I decided I for sure wouldn't get to play if I didn't at least try."

"That's the spirit!"

Understanding that they can choose behavior that will benefit them, as well as choose to avoid behaviors that will hurt them, is an exciting discovery. Personal responsibility is actually a powerful motivator and gives young people a sense of self-control and participation in their own destiny.

4. PRACTICE SELF-CONTROL

A fourth fundamental to success in the game of life is self-control, not acting impulsively simply based on emotions. But that's difficult, and we must be taught how to exercise self-control. In athletics, if we're unable to control ourselves emotionally, we are going to be a detriment to ourselves and to our team. The same is true in the game of life.

If you follow professional sports, you might remember Latrell Sprewell, a talented young man with the Golden State Warriors, who, in a moment of frustration, choked his coach, P. J. Carlissimo. This incident received national and worldwide attention and initiated a debate about young people being able to control their emotions and avoid behavior that would be harmful to themselves and others. Suspended for most of the season, Sprewell lost millions of dollars for his action.

Dennis Rodman, the outrageous former Chicago Bull, fell on top of a cameraman, causing an injury to the star's leg. In frustration, Rodman lashed out and kicked the cameraman in the groin. This incident cost Rodman suspension from the team, several thousand dollars in fines, and hundreds of thousands more in a lawsuit. Lack of self-control can be very costly.

If the players of your favorite sports team have no self-control and start behaving in a way that causes the team to lose games, what will be your first reaction as a fan? You expect the coach to get his team under control, and if that doesn't happen, you are soon asking for a new coach.

As parents, it is our responsibility to coach our kids in the game of life—and that includes their emotional self-control.

Give kids practice in self-control. One thing we do at the Byrdsong household is pay very little attention to the typical teasing that goes on among our kids ("Maaaaa! He's looking at me!"). When we do respond, we focus more on the reactions of the kid who's being teased than on the one who's doing the teasing. (Tattling, screaming, hitting, and throwing things are not appropriate

> Always keep your composure. . . . You can't score from the penalty box, and to win, you have to score.
>
> —*Bobby Hull, NHL left wing*

reactions to teasing. Keeping a sense of humor, ignoring, or leaving the room are more appropriate responses.) It helps our kids learn how we expect them to behave when they feel they are in an adverse situation outside the home. When they're teased or picked on at school, it would still be inappropriate for them to strike out at the perpetrator.

Don't reward out-of-control behavior. Why don't kids learn self-control? Because being out of control "works"! Ever see Molly Mophead throwing a royal tantrum in the grocery store because Mama said she couldn't have Choco-Frosted Pops cereal? What happens next? Mama gives in and says, "OK, I'll buy the cereal, but just this once." She has just rewarded Molly's misbehavior—and you can believe it's going to happen again.

The language we use can also reinforce kids' emotionally immature behavior. If Willie comes home after hitting someone at school, and you hear about it, what is your reaction? You may ask, "What did he do to you?" The message is, *my* kid's not responsible; someone must have *made* him act this way. This type of language allows kids to believe losing their self-control is justified; it's someone else's fault that they got mad. But a more appropriate line of questioning would be "What happened? What other choices did you have besides hitting in response to what the other person did?" Our goal as parents is to help our young people realize that regardless of how they feel, they can choose an appropriate response to what happens to them.

Inappropriate responses need appropriate consequences. When a player loses control of his emotions in the game of basketball, the official gives the player a technical foul. Now, we all understand that emotions can run high in a game. Things happen. But it doesn't matter if a player is frustrated, has his space violated, or is disrespected. The official cannot excuse wrong responses. The technical foul is a reminder: practice self-control.

If someone on an opposing team did or said something that provoked one of my players to throw the ball in disgust and get a technical foul, my first comment to the player was not, "What did he say to you?" Instead, I would say, "You can't throw the basketball into the stands when you're mad." I would tell him I saw what happened and understood that he was angry, but I wanted him to get the message that acting out his anger is not an appropriate response.

Whether we're coaching a sports team or coaching the family team, we need to be giving our young people the message: Life is full of things that make us frustrated and angry; learning self-control may make the difference between success in life and a lifetime of regret. To get the message across, we may need to dole out a consequence (time-out, loss of privilege, or other related discipline) for their giving in to inappropriate behavior, regardless of the emotional justification. Unfortunately our prisons are full of "good kids" who are there for the simple reason that they never learned self-control and made a wrong decision during the height of their emotions.

Help kids learn appropriate responses. Generally when we talk about emotions and self-control we think of anger. But there are other emotions we need to consider also: feelings of rejection, sadness, depression; even happiness or excitement (as in the riots that have occurred when a city's team has won a championship). We certainly don't want our kid taking a gun to school and shooting someone because he is despondent over breaking up with his girlfriend.

Emotions are powerful, but we parents need to help our children learn to handle them appropriately. This may include:

- *Listening* to our children and hearing how they feel.
  ("Want to tell me about it?")
- Accepting their feelings as *feelings*.
  (Don't say, "Of course you don't hate your teacher! What a terrible thing to say.")
- Helping them talk about and *test their perceptions*.
  ("Why do you think she doesn't like you?")
- Encouraging them to *not act on initial feelings*, but to allow time to think through the larger picture.
  ("Write down what you'd like to say, but hang onto it and see how you feel about it after the weekend.")
- Giving them appropriate outlets for their feelings.
  ("Why don't you write down what you're feeling in your journal?" or "Let's go for a bike ride and let off some of that steam.")

Emotions are simply feelings—how we feel at the moment. Emotions may or may not reflect the true situation. We need to help our kids understand that these emotions often are based on how we perceive things, which may change with time or additional information. It's important to teach our kids self-control, so that they are able to think through the larger picture.

5. ENCOURAGE A POSITIVE MENTAL ATTITUDE

A fifth fundamental to success is a positive mental attitude. You've heard the phrase, "A winning attitude." The "wisdom" book in the Bible says, "As [a person] thinketh in his heart, so is he."[5] If a person thinks of

---

[5]*Proverbs 23:7, the Holy Bible.*

himself as a loser, he'll be a loser. A sports team that doesn't have the confidence that they can beat their opponents, probably won't. Someone who thinks the whole world is against him will surely find lots of things to complain about.

On the other hand, a young person determined to get through college probably will. A young man or woman with a positive attitude will see obstacles as challenges—turning "lemons into lemonade." So much of what we do or accomplish depends on that inner attitude.

At first glance, a positive mental attitude may sound a lot like healthy self-esteem, but the two are different. Healthy self-esteem is primarily how a person feels about himself or herself. A positive mental attitude, on the other hand, tends to be a broader picture of how this person feels about life in general. I personally believe it's important to have a positive view about life in general. As a parent, I want to help my children understand that life is exciting, life has a lot of possibilities.

But it wasn't always this way.

I spent my boyhood in Atlanta, Georgia. I love Atlanta. It's a very friendly and progressive city. However, there was a time in Atlanta, as in many other places in our nation, when racism was much more out in the open than it is today. I remember walking down the street and hearing white youths drive by calling out, "Nigger!" I had to think twice about where I went and what I did, because black folks weren't always made to feel welcome. From early on, my mental attitude was rather negative; I thought my chances for success in life were slim because of racism.

But I had a teacher who taught me to look at these experiences differently, and it changed my whole perspective on life. She told me that the people who called me names did so to boost their own self-importance by putting other people down. It was more a reflection of their ignorance than a reflection on me. Two or three kids in a car acted that way, not all of America. This teacher also introduced me to other blacks who had been successful in life, even against great odds. She helped change my perspective, which has helped me maintain a positive attitude about life even when I face obstacles.

We must give our kids perspective. It would be detrimental for me as a parent to foster the attitude that "life just isn't fair," because that attitude serves no good purpose. We can be honest about the obstacles our kids will face in life, encouraging them to find a way around those obstacles. To validate complaints like "Life isn't fair" or "All white people are racist" or "You'll never get past the glass ceiling" is harmful to our children's ability to develop a positive mental attitude. We need to point to men and women who have overcome and who did so by heading into the various challenges in their life.

When I was coaching, my players' first reaction when we lost a game was often that "the officials were biased." The coaching staff was quick to not allow this type of thinking to get a foothold. We had to maintain confidence that the game was being played fairly and that the four or five mistakes *we* made were the reason we were not successful. Why? If we blamed it all on "biased officials," we lost control of the outcome. *Admitting our own mistakes and finding ways to correct them allowed us to maintain a positive attitude, because we were in control. We could change the outcome.*

When our kids feel frustrated about setbacks or disappointments in their life, asking some key questions might help them gain perspective: "Are there other ways of looking at what happened? Can we still be successful in spite of what happened? Is this a roadblock or a detour? Is there another way to get there?"

Failure can be a stepping-stone. None of us likes to fail. But some people are so afraid of failure that they won't even try! If they don't try, they can't fail. But anybody who has become somebody has experienced setbacks and failures along the way. How many times do you think Thomas Edison tried and "failed" before he invented the light bulb? As parents, we need to help our children reevaluate what failure really is and give them a new perspective: *The only real failure is not trying.*

We also need to ask what kinds of signals we're sending our kids about what's important. What do we value most: winning at all costs, or how the game is played? When I was coaching, there were nights when we won the game but I was not happy with how my team had played. I couldn't honestly say, "Great game," just because we won. Likewise, at home, if your kids are pulling off good grades, but you feel deep down that they're not putting forth their best effort or "studying to learn," you will need to focus on effort more than on result. At the same time, if your kids come home with C's on their report card, but you feel the effort was strong, you can show tremendous pride in that.

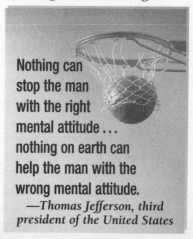

Nothing can stop the man with the right mental attitude . . . nothing on earth can help the man with the wrong mental attitude.
—*Thomas Jefferson, third president of the United States*

Positive thinking isn't a magic formula. I'm not saying that a positive mental attitude will allow us to accomplish everything we attempt to do. But it can give us the motivation to do the things that *we* need to do. My daughter Sabrina needs to work on her free-throw shooting, but if she doesn't think she can improve her throw, it's going to impact her level of trying. Even though she works at it, she won't be as effective as she could be if she thought it was possible. *Positive thinking allows us to put forth the appropriate effort.*

Zig Ziglar, a well-known motivational speaker and author, summed it up this way: "Positive thinking won't let you do everything, but it will let you do everything better than negative thinking will."

6. PROMOTE COURAGE

Just as a positive mental attitude gives kids the courage to try, and not be afraid of failure, *courage to face adversity is fundamental to success in the game of life.* We parents won't always be there to protect our children from the difficult challenges they will face in life, but we really hurt our kids if we always run to the rescue and don't give them a chance to solve their own problems.

Recently I watched my son, Ricky, play in a hockey game. I thought one of the kids on the opposing team was purposely physical with him, throwing elbows and cheap shots. Sure, I was tempted to call out to the official and point out what this kid was doing, but I held back and didn't say anything. I wanted to give my kid a chance to decide for himself how he would handle the situation. And, sure enough, a few minutes into play I saw Ricky elbow this kid in the stomach, and for the rest of the match that kid avoided him. I don't encourage aggressive play, but the bottom line was that I didn't want to step in and rescue my kid and fight his battles for him.

Our kids *will* encounter adverse situations—whether it's the neighborhood bully picking on smaller kids, or kids passing vicious rumors around the school, or someone pressuring them to take a drink or try a smoke—and we need to help equip them to fight their own battles. We can help by encouraging them to stand up for themselves and what they believe in, but also by suggesting guidelines for assessing a situation and showing them what options they have for handling the problem: When do they speak up? Defend themselves? Walk out? Get help from an adult?

There is a larger reason why our kids need courage to do the right thing. Two hundred years ago a wise British statesman said, "The only thing necessary for the triumph of evil is for good men to do nothing."[6] As parents, we want our children not only to look out for their own interests but also the interests of others. But first we parents have to model that kind of courage.

Recently our family, along with several other families, walked through a neighborhood in our hometown of Evanston. This neighborhood was troubled by drugs, alcohol, gang activity, divorce, hurting families—things that trouble many neighborhoods across our nation. We ended up stopping on the sidewalk and praying aloud for the neighborhood in general. My three kids were surprised that we would stop and pray while people were watching. Admittedly it took a certain amount of courage not to care what people thought. But our children need to see their parents act on what they believe, speak out against things that are wrong, speak up on behalf of the needs and rights of others. If we do so, we are planting seeds of courage in their own hearts.

INSTANT REPLAY

These are the "skills" that I feel are the most fundamental if our kids are going to win in the game of life. Some of you may be surprised that I didn't mention "education" as fundamental to success. (We'll deal with that in chapter 6.) Don't get me wrong. A good education is extremely important. But I tend to look at "fundamentals" as the keys that open the doors to everything else. Each of the fundamentals I've mentioned is essential to *making use of the opportunities* that lead to success. Is it possible for a child to be educated if he lacks self-control, obedience, a positive mental attitude, and self-esteem? Chances are that an unruly, disobedient child lacks a "teachable spirit." If he lacks self-esteem he'll be an underachiever. Without a positive mental attitude and courage, he may lack the motivation to make the most of the opportunities available to him.

Rather than expending all our energy making sure that our kids get into the most expensive schools, let's make sure our kids are *obedient*, possess a healthy *self-esteem*, practice personal *responsibility* and *self-control*, develop a *positive mental attitude*, and exercise *courage*.

With these fundamentals, now we're ready to make a game plan.

---

[6]Attributed to Edmund Burke (1729–1797).

FREE THROW

1. Develop healthy self-esteem

It may seem contradictory to say that children need both to be accepted *for who they are, not for what they can do,* and they need to *experience a sense of competence,* the satisfaction of doing something well. Nonetheless, both ingredients are essential for a healthy self-esteem.

Look at the following list of comments. Put a plus sign (+) in front of the ones that help promote healthy self-esteem, and a minus sign (-) in front of the ones that create anxiety and insecurity.

____ 1. "Why can't you be more like your brother?" ____

____ 2. "Oh, I love you so much for cleaning up the playroom!" ____

____ 3. "You cleaned up the playroom? Nice job!" ____

____ 4. "I love you." ____

____ 5. "When you were born, your mommy and I were so excited!" ____

____ 6. "You call that making your bed? Here, let me do it." ____

____ 7. "No school today? Oh no—you kids drive me crazy." ____

____ 8. "Hey, let's go out for ice cream, just you and me." ____

____ 9. "You've been a big help today. I really appreciate it." ____

____ 10. "Why can't you do something right for a change?" ____

____ 11. "Don't worry about it. We all make mistakes." ____

____ 12. "Oh, yes, we're proud of Zoe. She's the smartest kid in her class." ____

____ 13. "I like that painting. You've got your own style." ____

____ 14. "You tried. That's what counts. I'm proud of you for sticking with it." ____

Now go back, and at the end of each plus (+) comment, put an *A* for comments that give a sense of acceptance; a *B* for a sense of belonging; a *C* for a sense of competence. The answer key is found in the footnotes.[7]

---

[7]ANSWER KEY: Positive comments: 3, 4, 5, 8, 9, 11, 13, 14. Negative comments: 1, 2, 6, 7, 10, 12. Comments that give Acceptance: 4, 11, 14; Belonging: 5, 8; Competence: 3, 9, 13. Are you surprised that #2 and #12 are listed as negative comments? If we tell our children we love them because of something they *did,* that causes them to be insecure. ("If I don't clean the playroom, will Mommy still love me?") Or if we brag too much about our kids being the smartest or fastest or best, what happens if someone comes along who is smarter or faster or better? Will we stop being proud of them?

2. Teach personal responsibility

Are you always rescuing your children? Or do you give them choices and let them experience the consequences of their choices?

From the following scenarios, *check* √ what you would normally do in that situation. Then *circle* the response that would most likely teach personal responsibility. Is there a difference between what is checked and what is circled?

(1) Your twelve-year-old daughter dashes off to school and forgets her lunch. Do you . . .
    a. drop her lunch off at school on your way to work?
    b. give her a lecture when she gets home?
    c. do nothing?

(2) You told your son to mow the lawn before he goes to the beach with his friends.
    a. You see that it's not getting done, so you nag him all morning about doing it.
    b. The lawn isn't mowed by the time his friends arrive, so you tell him he has to do it as soon as he gets back from the beach.
    c. The lawn isn't mowed by the time his friends arrive, so you tell him he can't go to the beach.

(3) Your teenager wants to get her driver's license. Do you . . .
    a. add her name to your insurance and let her drive the family car?
    b. buy her a new car and pay for the insurance?
    c. tell her she can drive the family car as soon as she can pay for the difference in your insurance?
    d. buy her a used car, but let the insurance, gas, and upkeep be her responsibility?

(4) Your six-year-old wants a puppy. Do you . . .
    a. buy one and begin doing all the care yourself?
    b. tell him that he is too young to own a dog?
    c. suggest he start with a goldfish or a hamster?
    d. have your son use some of his money to buy the dog and begin by teaching him to take some of the responsibility for its care?

(5) Your sixteen-year-old daughter wants a $65 pair of Oliver sun-
    glasses. ("Well, it's not like I'm asking for the $115 Gucci
    pair or those cool ones by Porsche for $272!") What do you say?
    a. Forget it!
    b. Tell her she can use her clothes allowance for them if she wants
       to, but you won't be bailing her out later.
    c. Deliver a lecture about conspicuous consumption and hunger in
       underdeveloped countries.

5. SCOUTING THE ENEMY'S COURT

Scouting.

The word conjures up images of whisker-faced frontiersmen sporting leather fringes, pushing alone into the wilderness to discover the best trail for the wagon train. Or maybe a squad of infantrymen creeping behind enemy lines to scout out the foe's vulnerable flank.

Success or failure. Smart scouting can make all the difference.

Scouting the enemy's court is a critical ingredient in good coaching. In 1993, just before Christmas, Holy Cross University was coming to town to play our Wildcats at Northwestern University. We were on a six-game winning streak, and if we could just go home on break undefeated, it might give us enough momentum to have our best year yet.

But Holy Cross's top player was Rob Feaster. In fact, he was the leading scorer in the Patriot League and number two in all of Division One. We didn't think we could win if we couldn't stop Feaster. We watched films for hours and looked for some clue about Feaster's game that would give us an advantage, but we couldn't find a thing. This really surprised us. Almost every player does things unconsciously that telegraph what he intends to do next. When we discover those patterns, we can defend against them. But with Feaster, we couldn't see a thing.

Then suddenly Shawn Parrish, one of my assistants, noticed that when Feaster dribbled the ball twice and picked it up, he would go up for a jump shot. But if he dribbled it three or more times before picking it up, he would pass it. The more we watched the more we could see that this pattern held true almost every time.

So we devised a strategy. If Feaster dribbled twice and then picked the ball up, our defender needed to jump to block his shot, because he was surely going to take one. But if he kept the ball down for three dribbles, we didn't have to worry about blocking a jump shot; we should look for the pass.

At game time, we blocked Feaster's first shot. That threw him off his rhythm for the rest of the game! It was Feaster's lowest scoring game of the year, and we won decisively—90 to 64. It created the momentum we needed to come back after Christmas break and win two more straight for a nine-game streak, leading Northwestern to its best season in eleven years.

It was amazing!

As a parent, don't you wish you could scout what your kids will face that effectively? Admittedly, that was an unusual situation. Rarely in basketball—let alone in life!—does one discover such useful clues. Still, we all want to know what's coming, whether it's the weather so we know how to dress, or who's on the phone before we pick it up, or which route we should take to avoid highway construction delays. We want that small edge so we won't be taken by surprise. And the more critical our venture, the more we want to know what's coming next.

There is probably no greater responsibility each of us has undertaken than parenting, guiding a young life into the future. Why shouldn't scouting be one of the prime tasks in helping our children avoid disastrous surprises? But how?

1. KNOW WHO THEY'RE WITH AND WHAT THEY'RE DOING

What? you say. Byrdsong, you're crazy! Have you ever tried keeping up with a teenager firing on every cylinder?

I know. Easier said than done. As a basketball coach, I was expected to do the same for thirteen college-age players, some of whom were technically adults. But one stupid adventure off court by my players, and our whole program could unravel! I learned that the hard way.

After a good first year at Northwestern, my team slipped to a dismal

5–22 in 1994–95. First, we lost five starters from the previous year. That was bad enough, but at least it was natural attrition. But then we discovered that one of our team's most valuable players was gambling. We suspended him for six games. Ouch! But the more we investigated, the worse things looked. Finally the FBI was brought in and the U.S. attorney indicted our MVP and the team's leading three-point shooter with conspiring to fix three Big Ten games in 1995. They finally admitted accepting thousands of dollars to "hold back" in order to shave points off our potential scores to satisfy the predictions of gambling interests on the games' final outcomes.

I was shocked and deeply disappointed.

Try as we might—and we did—our team and even my career as head coach for Northwestern basketball never fully recovered from that scandal. Clearly I had not been keeping close enough tabs on my players! But should I have known? Was it my job to know what these young men were doing and with whom they were doing it 24–7?

Yes. As head coach, the buck stopped with me. And as parents, the buck stops with each one of us as long as our children live under our roof. I know that's a hard thing to say to a mother who suddenly discovers that her son is hooked on crack cocaine or to a father who finds that his daughter is pregnant by someone he doesn't even know. I know that it's a painful reality because of what I went through in the gambling scandal. But it is true. The buck stops with us! Accepting that responsibility may not guarantee success, but acceptance is essential if there is to be any hope for success.

> Like the rest of the country, we are struggling to understand why this happened.
>
> —*Parent of Dylan Klebold, teen shooter, Littleton, Colorado*

A myth has developed in our society that encourages parents to reject this responsibility. This myth claims that every child has a right to privacy as though he or she were an independent adult. I disagree. While it's proper to knock so that we don't walk in on our older children while they're dressing, and as a general rule we shouldn't open their mail or read their diaries, it is absolutely foolish to buy into the myth that children should lead a private life to which we have no entrance or knowledge. Who their friends are, where they go, what they do . . . it *is* our business, because we are responsible for their welfare.

But how do you accomplish this oversight? Here are some suggestions.

- Begin by establishing your oversight as your family's standard expectation. Again and again as your children grow up, verbally mention your policy: "I always expect to know where you are, whom you are with, and what you are doing." Let this be your standard operating procedure, not your response to some specific problem or suspicion. Before little Hannah goes out the door to play at Hilda's house, remind her: "If any plans change, just give Mommy a call."

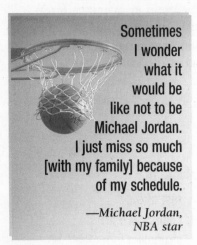

Sometimes
I wonder
what it
would be
like not to be
Michael Jordan.
I just miss so much
[with my family] because
of my schedule.

—*Michael Jordan,*
NBA star

- When those calls come, try to accommodate them as often as possible, and thank your child for keeping you informed so that this policy is not onerous. It's just the way you do things.
- Check up on your children from time to time. Again, don't make this an unpleasant event. For instance, you might stop by the park and tell Robbie, "I knew you were playing baseball here and were supposed to come home at three, but I thought I'd stop by to see if you wanted to stay until four."
- Affirm your child's cooperation with your policy. At the same time, make a big deal over violations—usually with loss of similar privileges for a short time.
- Let the parents of your children's friends know of your policy so that they can cooperate by checking with you if plans change when your child is in their care.
- Practice what you preach. Sooner or later your adolescent will accuse you of not trusting him or her. However, if you have consistently let your spouse and your children know where you are and when you'll be home—and call when you need to change plans—it is easier to explain your policy as "family courtesy." Your good example will make it easier for your budding adolescents to maintain

the practice even when they start wanting to be on their own. You are showing them that being an adult does not equal disregard for family order.

- Finally, maintain genuine interest in your kids' activities, troubles, and ideas—and ask lots of questions about those things.

Whenever my basketball players were with me, we discussed what was taking place off the court. "So what's going on tonight?" I'd ask. "Where are you going?"—particularly if it was a weekend and they were not studying. Whenever they mentioned a name that I didn't recognize, I'd say, "Hey, don't think I've had the pleasure. Does he come to the games? Why don't you have him stop by some time. I'd like to meet him."

This gave me an opportunity to get to know the people they knew, which in turn gave me more information about what was happening with my players when I was not with them. Once I got to know their friends, I often enlisted them in supporting my team members. For instance, if my player Mike was going out on the weekend with Melvin, I might say, "Hey, Mel. Make sure Mike is in by eleven tonight, because we have that important game two days from now and he needs the proper amount of rest." Somehow that made Mel feel like a part of the "team." The next time I saw him, I either thanked him or asked why he let the

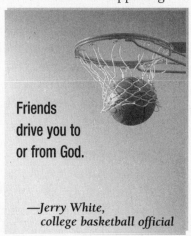

Friends drive you to or from God.

—*Jerry White,*
college basketball official

team down by not looking out for one of our players as I had asked! Soon I could tell who really kept the best interest of our players in mind, who were positive influences, and who were negative.

Parents, you can do the same thing with your kids. As soon as your kids start wanting to "go play at Elmo's house" (about age four or five), do some innocuous "scouting." Have Elmo come play at your house where you can observe him. Drop in and meet his parents. What do they do at Elmo's house? Do their values support your values?

Because my wife and I are very particular about what our kids watch on TV, we care about what they watch at their friends' houses. If the friends' parents don't share our standards, then we might not want our kids spending so much time at their house. Instead, we might arrange for most of their playtimes to occur at our house. Don't feel like you need to apologize for the things that you believe are best for your kids.

Having given all these suggestions, however, we must realize that a determined kid can circumvent our best efforts to monitor his or her behavior and associations. The gambling scandal that rocked Northwestern University proved this to me. I had no idea what was going on, and various players have since stated that there was no way I could have known. Nevertheless, it is healthy to evaluate our methods when things go wrong. I had made it my business to get to know my players' friends and associations. How could players on my team be gambling without my knowing about it? Why didn't I know the contact person who paid them off for throwing the games?

But the fact remains: If someone was intent on breaking the law behind my back, I couldn't *make* him do the right thing. And as a parent, you cannot force your older kids to behave if they are determined to defy your standards. But you *can* keep your standards high and follow up to guide them in the right direction.

It does no good to go on a guilt trip, but if your evaluation suggests a change in your approach, make it and move on with life. Blame tends to make things seem final, but evaluating helps us to approach life as a process.

2. KNOW THE HAZARDS

When I was coaching at the University of Arizona, our team was scheduled to play Oregon State. We knew from the statistics that the free-throw averages of visiting teams at Oregon State were unusually low. Visitors just couldn't hit free throws in their gym! There had to be a reason. So we scouted their games and discovered the reason, all right. Just before a visiting player shot a free throw, a kid right behind the basket would hold up a large poster of Farrah Fawcett in a bikini.

At first we laughed in disbelief, but that was their trick. We watched the tapes, and sure enough, every time the poster went up, their opponents' free-throw averages went down.

So we bought our own poster, and during practice we held up Farrah Fawcett. "Get it out of your system," we said. "Gawk now so that come the game, you won't be fazed." And it worked. Before long, our players were so used to the poster that it no longer distracted them. By knowing what hazards they would face, our boys shot their usual averages and we won the game.

What are the hazards your children will face? They will differ with age and locale, but here are two lists. The first suggests sources where you can gain intelligence. The second suggests some of the things you should watch for.

Where to Scout

- Attend PTA meetings and learn what your children will be taught— about family life, health, history, values, etc. If you are not comfortable with the content, make your concerns known. Suggest constructive alternatives or supplements.

- Attend all parent/teacher conferences so you have a clear idea of how your child is doing in school. In addition to asking about academic progress, get a good picture of how your child interacts with the other children. For younger children, you might want to visit the class occasionally yourself.

- Monitor your school and the basic problems within it. Ask questions of teachers, coaches, and the principal until you learn what their challenges are. Don't be mollified by answers like "Oh, most of our kids are fairly well behaved." Of course most are, and you trust your child is among that number, but you are trying to discover what else is out there.

- Whenever your local police have a neighborhood or citizens' meeting, attend it and ask lots of questions about what is happening with the youth in your community.

- Volunteer at your school. Often parents are welcome to help in the lunchroom or in before- and after-school programs. Volunteer to help chaperone on field trips and school dances—even if your child does not participate. The point is, you need to be familiar with the "court" (the youth culture) on which your child must "play."

- Ask your kids (possibly including some of their friends) what they know. What do other kids do after games? What happens at the school dances, outside the dance, and after the dance? What kinds of private parties are being thrown? What do kids do at them?

What kind of groups, cliques, gangs are in the school? Where do these groups hang out? What happens in the lunchroom, in the rest rooms, and what goes on off campus? What are the most dangerous places around school/town? Why? Your kids will probably talk freely about these things before they are involved in anything negative. But that's when you need to do your scouting.

• Talk to the parents of your kids' friends. At church or at school functions, talk to parents of kids a couple of years older than your own. What do they know about what's happening in your community?

What to Scout

• Almost every junior high and high school has a social landscape that includes snobs, jocks, partiers, gangs, nerds, cults (not necessarily religion, but consuming interests like heavy metal music, surfing, gaming, etc.), outcasts, loners, and even some "normal" kids that don't fit any of the other categories. Where does your kid fit into this landscape? With which groups does your kid feel the most empathy?

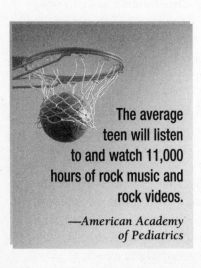

The average teen will listen to and watch 11,000 hours of rock music and rock videos.

—*American Academy of Pediatrics*

• What kinds of weapons have shown up at your kid's school? How frequently? What is the school doing about it?

• What kinds of drugs are most common in your community and your kid's school? Can you recognize these drugs and the symptoms of their use?

• Which gangs are in your school and community? Can you recognize their signs, colors, hand signals, or other symbols?

• As the saying goes, "Garbage in, garbage out!" What your kid feeds his or her mind on will influence who they become and how they behave. What are the lyrics of the music your young person listens to most? (The words are often printed with the liner notes.) What is the content of the videos he or she watches? (You'll have to watch these yourself.) What is the lifestyle of the celebrities they idolize most? (Pick up some teen magazines.)

3. KNOW YOUR KID'S STRENGTHS AND WEAKNESSES

When I was an assistant coach, my early scouting reports were elaborate. Whenever I saw a pattern in the opponent, I focused in on it and brought the information back so we coaches could prepare an effective game plan for our team.

But we couldn't dump everything on the kids. There are thousands of moves in a forty-minute basketball game. Every second there is a pass, a shot, someone dribbling behind their back. If I were to report every little thing that went on in a game, the team would be overwhelmed with the details and soon tune out or become fearful, and therefore unprepared. So I looked for patterns. Our coaching staff would then refine those down to the few moves we thought our team could take advantage of, either offensively or defensively. Those we worked into the game plan we presented to our team.

During my 1996–97 season at Northwestern University, Julian Bonner was a sophomore on our Wildcat basketball team. In practice he was outstanding, but come game time he seemed to play far below his potential. I watched him closely, and he was not negligent; he didn't make foolish or reckless moves. If anything, he seemed too cautious, too constrained, as though he couldn't let himself go.

Talking about it with the other coaches, we surmised that he was analyzing himself and the game so much that he couldn't play freely. We came up with a most unusual remedy: We asked him to listen to music on his Walkman for four hours prior to the next game to keep his mind from obsessing about how he was going to play.

He tried it, and we couldn't believe the improvement! It was dramatic. He played like he did in practice—even better. Pretty soon everybody on the team was listening to headphones before games. I don't know how much it helped some of the other players, but it was a breakthrough for Bonner. He went on to have a very fine college career.

As parents, in addition to scouting out the hazards our kids will face, we need to know how they are likely to respond to that information. Increased pressure may cause one child to rise to the challenge, while another will be overwhelmed. We need to know how much is good for each child.

You work to strengthen your weakest link, not to worry about the strongest one.

—Bum Phillips, NFL coach

In our schools and communities today there are drugs, alcohol, foul language, bullies, gangs, television, radio, video games, the Internet—the list goes on and on. You need to know about these pitfalls, but you have to make careful decisions about what you dump on your children, especially based on their age and sensitivity. We can point to all of these things and call them major distractions, but we must determine what things are most critical for our children. We may be able to shield our children from certain hazards, like a coach who doesn't call certain plays that would put his team in precarious situations. Among the dangers that remain, we need to select the three or four highest priorities to focus on based on what our kids might be most susceptible to and what they can handle. The things you select to emphasize should be based on the profiles you have developed of your kids from the "Free Throw" activity in chapter 3. For instance, what is/are

- the most effective long-run discipline for this child?
- the most effective short-term discipline for this child?
- the things that discourage this child?
- the things that motivate this child?
- the things that frighten this child?
- the way that this child copes with change?
- the way that this child handles extended routine?
- the way that this child responds to peer pressure?

4. DON'T JUST TELL 'EM, SELL 'EM

As parents, it's important that we don't merely *tell* our kids what we know from our scouting, we need to *sell* them on it. Often, as a coach, I noticed our players keyed into the things that we coaches felt were important based on our tone of voice and how we presented an issue. We would show them statistical proof that what we saw was so. We would return to a concern again and again. We would show videos. We left no doubt in their minds how seriously we took a concern.

You can do the same: bring counsel to your kids that you support by research, articles, the testimony of other people, and the intensity of your own concern. However, I have a couple of cautions:

(1) Don't overstate your case. The 1936 film *Reefer Madness* backfired in its effort to warn young people about the dangers of marijuana precisely because of its exaggerations. Kids soon realized that the use of marijuana did not end inevitably "in incurable insanity," as the film claimed. Consequently, it became a joke that young people used to dismiss all warnings about marijuana.

(2) Don't become a Johnny-one-note. There is a difference between reemphasizing something as needed and becoming a nag. If you can't let it alone, your kids will either conclude that you don't trust them or consider the issue so important that it attracts them simply because of your continual harping on it.

5. EFFECTIVE SCOUTING HAPPENS BEFORE THE GAME

There is a way to guide your kids in the "middle of the game" without lambasting them with "Why would you do something like that?!" (a sure way to turn them off). But frankly, we can be most effective in guiding our children when we do our scouting and apply what we've learned "before the game," so to speak. Here are some of the reasons.

Confidence comes from planning and practicing well.

—*Vince Lombardi,*
NFL coaching legend

• If you wait until you see them doing something you don't like and then try to stop it, you risk driving them further and further into that behavior. It's much more effective to point out things when there's no pressure, when no one is upset, and when you are basically sharing information.

• Warning them ahead of time gives them the opportunity to avoid the embarrassing experience of having to step back from something after they have already started it with or in front of their friends. They may not admit the value of this at the time, but do it the other way around, and you'll undoubtedly get the complaint,

"Why didn't you tell me beforehand that I couldn't do it?"

- Talking about it ahead of time also gives you a chance to deflate some of their arguments. Then you can say, "I know you are going to say that Marcy's parents let her watch R-rated videos all the time, but I've already considered that. I think it would be better for her and easier on you if she didn't watch them, but I'm not raising her. I'm responsible for you."

- We can forewarn our kids of some of the flak they might receive when they have to go against the crowd. For instance, warning your kids that some friends might pressure them to ride with someone who has been drinking will only make you appear more astute when they encounter that experience. And, hopefully, they will have had time to develop some resolve to do the right thing.

- Scouting increases your kids' confidence in your leadership when they see that you do know what is going on out there in their world. Hopefully, they will come looking for your advice more often.

INSTANT REPLAY

Near the end of our 1993–94 season at Northwestern University, the Wildcats were 13–13 going into our last game of the regular season. It was against Michigan, a long-standing national power. Michigan had recruited five of the nation's best players in one class (Juwan Howard, Jimmy King, Ray Jackson, Jalen Rose, and Chris Webber), and they had earned the nickname, the "Fab Five," so it was going to be a tough game.

But we had a lot on the line. If we could win, we would earn a berth in post-season play—for only the second time in Northwestern's history. But a Michigan win would give them a Big Ten Championship.

From our scouting reports we discovered that Michigan would double-team the post player every time he caught the ball. They would trap him so tightly that he could not make it to the basket side. Caught like this, most players typically fought like mad to break through, sometimes losing the ball, sometimes committing a foul, but seldom making it to the basket for a successful shot.

Once we figured out that pattern, we told our guy that whenever he caught the ball at the post, he should dribble it out to the corner, drawing the double team with him. That would always leave one of our other players unguarded on the other side of the court to receive a pass and try an open shot.

With so much on the line for both teams, the game was sold out. The pressure was on. When the final buzzer sounded, it was one of the biggest wins in Northwestern history! Steve Fisher, the head coach at Michigan, credited our victory to the way we played against the double team. "No one," he said, "ever played against our double team so effectively."

Scout your children's world. You'll not only be able to protect them from surprise attacks but you also will know better how to help them when they do get caught in a "double team."

FREE THROW

1. Thinking about your kid's strengths and weaknesses

On the following chart, begin in the middle, then decide whether your child tends to be a loner, a leader, or a follower. Then determine how he or she tends to play out that role.

- Leaders receive attention and affirmation from others, but what does your child do to get that affirmation or attention? Does it come more often by leading others into positive or negative activities?

- If your child is a follower, who are the kinds of people your child tends to follow? Leaders who engage in positive activities or negative activities?

- If your child tends to be a loner, how does that affect him or her? Is it experienced with contentment or with sadness or maybe even self-pity for being left out?

Most likely, none of these categories will be true consistently for your child. Even if your child usually follows a positive leader, for instance, there may be times when he or she goes along with something foolish.

The purpose of the chart is to help you consider how your children are likely to experience the hazards in *their* game of life. It might not be the same way these things would affect you if you were the same age.

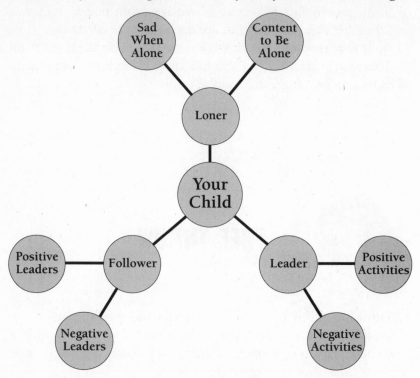

2. Determining the hazards your kids will face

Identify three areas you should research to understand the hazards your child will face. For each area, identify two places where you might find reliable information. For suggestions, see the sections "Where to Scout" and "What to Scout" earlier in this chapter.

(a) I am unsure what my child is likely to face regarding _____

_____

I might be able to find information from_____

_____

or _____

(b) I am unsure what my child is likely to face regarding _____
_____

I might be able to find information from_____
_____

or _____

(c) I am unsure what my child is likely to face regarding _____
_____

I might be able to find information from_____
_____

or _____

6. THE GAME PLAN

Sometimes in the game of life, it may seem as though other families have all the advantages—money, higher education, fancy titles after their names. They've got privilege, and they can give their kids whatever they want—or so it seems. They look like "Goliath" and we feel like puny "David." How are our kids ever going to win in a world with that kind of competition?

But in life, just as in basketball, a smart game plan is often more important than the "big advantages." Case in point:

All the experts said it would be a rout. Slower-paced Utah had no chance of defeating the run-and-gun offense of the defending NCAA champions from Arizona. After all, Arizona boasted All-Americans Mike Bibby and Miles Simon, not to mention hot shooter Michael Dickerson.

But when "David" met "Goliath" in the 1998 West Regional Championship playoffs, the smart game plan of the Utes handed the strong Arizona Wildcats one of their worst postseason losses ever: 76–51!

The game plan that Utah coach Rick Majerus pulled out of his bag was the risky and seldom-used triangle-and-two defense, which left the perimeter wide open. Had Arizona been on their game, they would have swamped Utah even worse than the experts had expected. But in watching the tapes, Majerus had seen something. He deployed his three back-line players in a triangle-shaped zone, while the guards played man-to-man. It was just enough to throw Mike Bibby off his stride, and that snowballed until Bibby was just 3 for 15, totaling seven points, while Simon and Dickerson were held to six points each.

In the meantime, five Utah players stepped up to hit double figures. "They beat us every way you can beat a team," admitted Arizona coach Lute Olson—but it all began with Utah's smart game plan.

A winning game plan must have two critical components: a good offense and a good defense. An *offense* is that part of the team effort designed to score points. You cannot win a game without scoring. The *defense* attempts to prevent your opponents from scoring points against you. There are teams that emphasize one strategy over the other—usually because of the expertise of the coaching staff. And sometimes those teams do well in the short run, especially if they come up with some unique techniques, but sooner or later the opponents of a lopsided team figure out a way to counteract their "specialty."

The Wright State Raiders from Dayton, Ohio, went into the first round of the 1993 NCAA tournament with an impressive height advantage over Indiana University. Three Raiders towered above Indiana's tallest at 6' 8". But Bobby Knight did not let appearances cow his Hoosiers. He coached them to run the legs off the tall boys. And that they did, winning 97 to 54! But the most amazing statistic out of the game was the fact that Indiana *out-rebounded* Wright State, 50 to 30. When fatigue neutralized the Raiders' "specialty," even that quit working for them.

Smart coach. Smart game plan.

In our families, our goal is no less than to create a comprehensive game plan that will enable our children to become champions in life. As the family coach, it is critical that the battle we prepare our kids to fight will be the one they actually face. If we've done our scouting and have a realistic idea of the challenges our kids will face, we can put together a strategy that takes into account our strengths and weaknesses as a family.

A balanced team that has developed both its offense and its defense has the strongest chance of prevailing. However, though the goal is balance, it is necessary to break that down and look at what it takes to create a strong offense and a strong defense.

A GOOD OFFENSE

Every good offense practices several ways to score. In basketball, there are lay-ups, dunks, fifteen-foot jumpers, free throws, three-point

shots, hooks, fadeaways, and a variety of other methods for putting that globe through the net. An effective offense will try to use all of these techniques to score. But before any of those shots can be effective, *the player has to be in a position to score.* If a player cannot find the lane to drive to the basket, then even a simple lay-up becomes improbable.

Location, location, location. In the game of life, putting your kid in a position to score involves more than geography!

The same would be true in the game of life. Before our kids can hope to score, we must coach them on how to get into *a position to score.*

Education

Education is the number one way to help your children be in position to score in the game of life. With a good education, your children will be in the best position to take advantage of the various opportunities that come along.

As a parent, *your* job is to see that your kids get that good education. But if it's not important to you, it won't be important to your kids.

When I bring special programs to various schools, I'm alarmed at the low participation of many parents. Parents tend to send their kids to school and then forget about them—until the school complains. Even at scheduled parent/teacher conferences, many parents don't show up. This is part of the reason why our kids don't take education more seriously! Why should they, if it means so little to their parents?

By getting involved, there is a lot you can do to improve your child's schooling. In some cases, you can help change the school for the better, but even where that is not possible, you can be sure your child gets the most out of what *is* available.

Where your local school district is not up to the task of providing a good education, you must do whatever is necessary to augment your kids' education. I like what one parent said when the subject of "public school" vs. "homeschool" was being discussed. She said: "*Every* parent is a homeschooler." It's true! What happens in the home should enlarge and enhance what happens during school hours.

Take the initiative. Spend time with your kids helping them with their homework; take them to the museum and the library; get them excited about reading. There are very few practical things in life that cannot be done and/or done better if one (1) knows how to find information, (2) can read well, and (3) can follow directions. On the other hand, people who cannot employ these three basic products of education will waste enormous amounts of time, energy, and money on the mere necessities of life—and still come up short. This includes everything from programming your VCR and managing your bank account to cooking a new recipe and maintaining your car so it will last as long as it should last.

Manhood, not scholarship, is the first aim of education.

—*Ernest Thompson Seton, Canadian writer*

Extracurricular Activities

Another way to position your kids so they can score in life is to involve them in extracurricular activities. Remember the old saying: "An idle mind is the devil's playground." It's worth considering, especially in an age in which there are so many negative influences vying for your child's attention.

My wife and I have made extracurricular activities an important priority for our children. When they finish their school day, they are involved in several other things that keep them busy. My oldest daughter, Sabrina, takes gymnastics and plays basketball; she also takes piano lessons and plays saxophone in the band. These enjoyable activities not only give her a sense of fulfillment but also give her an opportunity to explore different interests and help "position her" to score if one of them develops into a major skill or interest. My other daughter, Kelley, and my son, Ricky, are similarly involved in various activities.

Our primary purpose for encouraging extracurricular activities is "offensive," to give them experiences that will enrich them and position them to score, but they have "defensive" benefits as well. If my kids didn't have constructive things to do, they would be more likely to become involved in negative activities.

You may say that your child is not interested in any of the traditional or organized activities. But there is something that each kid *can* do, and as parents we need to discover what that is and encourage our child in his or her particular area of interest and ability. Is your child a "people person"? Maybe she would enjoy being a "mother's helper" or visit the elderly in a nursing home. Is your child more of a loner? Get him involved in woodworking, creating websites, cooking, or crafts. Does your child love animals? Volunteering at the local animal shelter or walking dogs for neighbors might be right up his or her alley. Is your child always clowning around? Harness his energy in children's theater, mime, or juggling. It will be worth it to you to do whatever is necessary to get your kids involved in constructive activities or projects.

I realize that for some parents, transportation to and from some of these activities can present a problem, but not all activities require an "at-home mom with a van." Ricky Jr. is in the chess club at school; he simply goes to school a little early on those mornings. If there aren't activities at your school, check out the local Boys or Girls Club, YMCA or YWCA, church or community activities.

Friendships

Don't underestimate the importance of solid friendships with wholesome peers to help put your kids in a position to score in the game of life. When I was coaching, the students who got into trouble almost always did so in the company of someone else. Very few kids get into trouble entirely on their own. This doesn't excuse them for their bad choices—everyone is responsible for their own decisions—but the influence of peers does make an impact for good or for ill.

So, how can we help our kids find and keep good friends? One of the things I recommend, even though it is sometimes quite challenging, is to *make your home the one where kids want to congregate*. Hoops in your driveway or alley or Nintendo in your basement are far easier to supervise than what goes on at the park or in someone else's home—especially if no adult is around at the other places. Offer to hold the party or sleepover at your house. Stock up on kid-friendly snacks that kids can share with their friends after school. Facilitating the entertainment of kids in your home goes a long way toward knowing *who* your kids are with, *where* they are, and *what* they're doing.

And when you think about getting together with friends, don't just get together as "couples" or as "girlfriends" or "the guys." Invite families with kids your kids' ages for an evening of games or a backyard cookout. If you like to go camping or have a favorite vacation spot, invite another family to join you. These activities and outings will give your children positive friendship experiences with other kids in a family context.

Something I really appreciate about my wife is how she makes the effort to get acquainted with the parents of our kids' friends. She knows them well and has developed friendships with them. If problems arise, the parents can talk. I recommend this to every parent. It is worth the time and effort. Your kids are important enough that you maintain a link to all the people who impact their lives.

A Solid Faith (a Religious Foundation)

And finally, one of the ways that we can put our children in a position to score is by taking them (not sending them) to a good church. "What's the surest guarantee that [a] . . . youth will not fall to drugs or crime?" asks a *U.S. News* cover story:

> Regular church attendance turns out to be a better predictor than family structure or income, according to a study by Harvard University economist Richard Freeman. Call it the "faith factor." The link between religious participation and avoidance of drug abuse, alcoholism, crime and other social pathologies is grist for some intriguing new research. Says Brookings Institution political scientist John Dilulio, "It's remarkable how much good empirical evidence there is that religious belief can make a positive difference." Policy makers are loath to promote faith because of their intellectual bias, he argues. But in most inner cities, where government, schools and other institutions fail the poor, says Dilulio, it is church programs that are "leveraging 10 times their own weight and solving social problems for us." And they offer personal salvation. A survey by John Gartner of Loyola College of Maryland and David Larson of Duke University Medical Center found over 30 studies that show a correlation between religious participation and avoidance of crime and substance abuse.[1]

---

[1]Joseph P. Shapiro with Andrea R. Wright, "The Faith Factor: Can Churches Save America?" *U.S. News* (September 9, 1996).

A church with a good education program not only gives our children a solid understanding of right and wrong but it also places them in the midst of a group of people who will be a second line of reinforcement for you as the parent. Other families and caring adults will get to know your children and become role models for them, someone else to cheer them on, counsel them, and look out for their well-being.

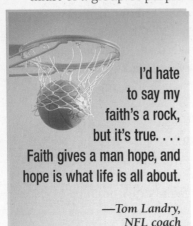

> I'd hate
> to say my
> faith's a rock,
> but it's true. . . .
> Faith gives a man hope, and
> hope is what life is all about.
>
> —*Tom Landry,*
> *NFL coach*

I mentioned earlier that involvement in church helped keep my wife and me married, not based alone on the sermons we heard from Sunday to Sunday, but because of the support we received during difficult periods in our lives. This same dynamic can help you and your kids.

Also, church involvement puts our kids in contact with others their own age who are more likely to be striving for the same values that you would like to see your kids have. But probably the most important asset is a *commitment to righteous living.* God calls us to live righteously. When we respond in faith, it is part of the package. It provides one more motivation to "do the right thing" when faced with a choice. But practicing faith comes with a warning. If *you* do not take God seriously in your life, it is unlikely that your children will exceed your godliness. In fact, they may come to scorn religious appeals to righteous living.

Therefore, *faith, if it is to be passed along, must be anchored in the home.* It is not enough to send our kids to church, or even to take them there. Your personal faith must be genuine if you want to pass it on to your children. Reading the Scriptures, family prayer, "living your faith" in your personal life—all these take faith out of the sanctuary and into your kids' everyday lives.

Now, you tell me: What do you believe the chances for success would be if your children had these four shots in their offensive game plan: a good education, extracurricular activities, wholesome friends, and a consistent life of faith? I believe you would agree that a young person possessing these four offensive tools stands a tremendous chance of being successful in the game of life.

A GOOD DEFENSE

We began this chapter noting that even the strongest offense wouldn't be enough if we didn't have a good defense. We need a plan to prevent our four areas of offense from being eroded. What inhibits or erodes a good education? What gets in the way of healthy extracurricular activities? What discourages good friendships? What will keep your child from developing a strong faith and participating eagerly in a good church?

Negative Peers

No wise parent wants to see his or her kids hanging out with people who are likely to encourage negative behavior. But all too often it sneaks up on us. We don't realize that the colors our kids insist on wearing or not wearing or the strange signals they make with their hands reflect an emerging gang affiliation.

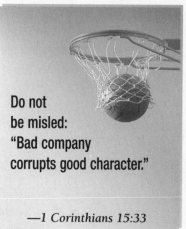

Do not be misled: "Bad company corrupts good character."

—1 Corinthians 15:33

We've said that a good *offense* would be to encourage your child's positive friendships. Obviously a good *defense* involves discouraging those friendships that might be unhealthy for your kids. But it is not always so easy to know the difference, and it can be even more difficult to intervene in a friendship. If you've tried, be assured you aren't the only parent who's been told, "You can't tell me who to like or not like."

Still, we must be aware of who our kids are involved with, and at the first sign of behaviors or attitudes we disapprove of, we need to address the issues respectfully but directly. This includes the use of offensive language, disrespect for adults, bad manners, cruelty, or anything you consider a deterrent to the development of your own child's good character. If the friend responds positively to your correction, then you have not only helped your own child but you have also added to the life of the friend.

A word of caution. While paying close attention to negative behavior and attitudes that might make some friendships unacceptable, do not allow your children to become snobs. When the Bible says, "*Bad* company corrupts good character," it does not mean *poor* company, or *unpopular* company, or *unsophisticated* company will corrupt good character. In fact, Jesus was the preeminent friend to the poor, to outcasts, even to sinners, and He despised the proud, the haughty, and the self-righteous. Therefore, you will do well to encourage your children to befriend the friendless. Your "defense" should kick in only when you encounter truly negative behavior and attitudes.

Television

A few years ago, African-American educator Jawanza Kunjufu said,

> At some point we're going to have to acknowledge that 72,000 hours of television—which shows 200,000 acts of violence and 25,000 sexual encounters outside of mar-riage— . . . 10 hours of videos a week and listening to 20 hours of rap, the billions of dollars spent advertising liquor and cigarettes on billboards, and over 10 billion dollars spent on an ad budget between television, radio, and print has to have some effect on shaping our values.[2]

Fortunately as a society we are starting to pay attention. The tobacco industry has been forced to accept that its advertising has encouraged dangerous addiction, and many studies have demonstrated that violence in games and movies can influence some kids to act violently. But even if the content of everything on television were positive, the amount of time most kids spend passively in front of the tube or glued to video games takes them away from the positive "offensive" activities we'd like them to pursue—education, extracurricular activities, solid friendships, and a good church life. TV tends to block us from having the opportunity to excel in those areas.

But there is an even subtler role the media plays in molding our youth. Stephen Glenn, author of *Raising Self-Reliant Children in a Self-Indulgent World* and internationally recognized expert on developing capable people, has said,

> The more hours of television children and adults watch, we've found the more pessimistic and deterministic they are in life—and the more they look at themselves and say, "Since I'm not big and powerful, why bother—I have no

---

[2]Jawanza Kunjufu, *Hip-Hop vs. MATT* (Chicago, Ill.: African American Images, 1993), 73.

control. Since I don't have those assets, I don't matter." We've raised a generation of young people who, rather than being involved in meaningful things, in families, in institutions, spend more of their childhood watching the media— a media that overwhelms them, defeats them, and gives them invalid role models.[3]

Another hazardous quality of the media is the way it tends to separate family members. Families don't tend to participate together. One kid likes one TV program; the other kids fight over the video games; Dad wants to watch sports; Mom checks out and does something else entirely.

Until recently we did not turn on our TV Monday through Thursday, and our kids could watch TV only on Friday, Saturday, and Sunday during the day. Even then we monitored the type of programs they watched. That's how our kids had enough time to do all their extracurricular activities. Recently we modified our plan to allow TV for brief periods each day because our kids were doing so well with their chores and homework. But we will be monitoring whether it cuts into their more productive activities.

However, I want to emphasize that if you decide to take something away from your children, be careful to always have something positive with which to replace it. Don't leave your kids with a vacuum. For instance, it was easy for us to keep the TV turned off Monday through Thursday, because we offered so many positive activities in its place.

Music

What kind of music do your children listen to? What did you like to listen to when you were young, and what did your parents think of it? I ask these two questions because it is quite natural for generations to differ in musical taste. The wise parent will not reject another generation's music simply because of style. However, there is far more to be examined than style. Just as it was with "our music," there are also the lyrics and the message modeled by the performers to be considered. If you look around, you'll notice how frequently many kids are wearing headphones. Those headphones may save you from being bombarded by a style of music you don't like, but they will not save your kids from any negative content that might be there.

---

[3]Stephen Glenn, "The Second Birth Called Adolescence," Youth Worker Update (Winter 1994): 60–61.

It's incumbent on parents to supervise what their kids are listening to and pay attention to how constantly it is feeding their minds—especially if its message is negative.

You've got to *be informed*! Remember: Garbage in, garbage out! If something is constantly being fed into the minds of your kids, it will have a tremendous impact on their behaviors and attitudes. If from an early age they listen to music that advocates extramarital sex, violence, revenge, drugs and alcohol, and degrades women, it stands to reason that they will be more inclined toward these behaviors and attitudes. What should shock and repulse them will seem natural, possibly even glamorous.

Again, I am not talking about style. I am talking about the content of the message, the example of the artists, the quantity of exposure . . . and whether your kids are mature enough to distinguish between something they like—which might be OK in itself—and a lot of other negativity associated with it. By that I mean, it takes substantial maturity for a kid to say, "I like that song, but I reject what the artist stands for and most of his or her other works."

Northwestern University, where I coached basketball, has as its motto a passage from the Bible:

> Whatsoever things are true,
>   whatsoever things are honest,
> Whatsoever things are just,
>   whatsoever things are pure,
> Whatsoever things are lovely,
>   whatsoever things are of good report;
> If there be any virtue, and
>   if there be any praise,
> Think on these things.[4]

A major university has recognized this as wise advice for young people. We would do well as parents to be on the alert as to what kinds of things are filling our children's minds.

So, read the words in the CD cases of your kids' music (if you can't decipher them by listening). Pick up a teen music magazine often enough to know who the popular artists are, what they advocate, and

---

[4]Philippians 4:8, the Holy Bible.

how they live. If you are an informed parent and talk to your kids early enough, they will respect your knowledge. What they won't respect—even if they obey you—is your yelling at them, "Turn that noise off! I can't stand it anymore!" Maybe you can't stand it, and you certainly deserve a break from something you don't like, but that's not a basis for teaching your children a strong defense against negative influences.

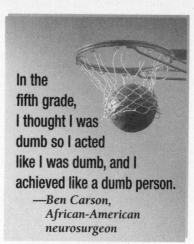

In the fifth grade, I thought I was dumb so I acted like I was dumb, and I achieved like a dumb person.
—*Ben Carson,*
African-American
neurosurgeon

Idle Time

The danger of too much idle time is the very reason I earlier urged the offensive weapon of an abundant extracurricular schedule. I also mentioned the adage, "An idle mind is the devil's playground." But why is that so? What are we defending against? Can't we just "chill out" and let our kids do as they please for a few years? They're young only once and schedules and responsibilities will all too soon rule their lives. Why not let 'em play?

If your children are the kind who initiate constructive, imaginative play, more power to them—provided there is some adult oversight. Play is, after all, the work of children. But a child who is busy playing is not "sogging" in idle time. He or she is busy. It's the idle time, the boredom, the purposelessness, and, finally, the chance for worthlessness to creep in that is the danger.

Several educators have told me that most teenage pregnancies and most gang involvement can be traced to those few hours between when school's out and when parents get home from work. In other words, unsupervised time without things to do has created a ripe environment for kids to get involved in destructive behaviors.

Parents, it is absolutely necessary for you see to it that your kids are not idle. And don't be fooled simply because your kids are "so nice" that they would never get into trouble. I've got a good friend who leads weekly Bible studies in the Cook County Juvenile Detention Center. He tells me that some of the nicest, politest, most gifted kids he has ever met have murder charges hanging over their heads simply because they got involved in something they didn't understand during periods of idleness.

You must make it a part of your game plan to make sure that when you are at work or otherwise occupied, your children are adequately involved in constructive and supervised activities. Supervision can range from a responsible adult simply being present and watching over what's going on to actual guided activities. If an occasional time arises when you can't arrange for trustworthy oversight by another adult, then at least you need to be making constant phone calls home to check on what's happening. Maybe you can have one of your friends stop in to see what is going on or have your children go over to your friend's house until you get home.

Don't be afraid that your kids will think less of you for making these arrangements. Some kids may scream that you don't trust them, but that is not the issue. The issue is: Are you being a responsible parent or not? Are you taking responsibility for all that your children are doing? Far more tragic are the kids that shrug and say, "My parents don't care what I do."

Most parents are very concerned about keeping their kids away from drugs, alcohol, and gangs, but if they would devote more attention to avoiding idle time, negative peers, and unwholesome media saturation, they would discover that their children were better defended against these problems that frighten parents so much.

IMPLEMENTING AN EFFECTIVE STRATEGY

A good offense and a good defense are the backbone of a balanced game plan for your children. But in order to have an effective strategy for coaching your kids to win at the game of life, your game plan must have two additional components. You must *schedule worthy opponents* for your team, and you must prepare them to *handle the unexpected*.

Scheduling Tough, Worthy Opponents

There are two ways coaches tend to schedule opponents. Some like to schedule easy opponents hoping to build an impressive record of wins. They may feel that their kids need a confidence boost, but this is a very dangerous strategy because sooner or later the team will have to face those tough opponents. If they are not ready for stiff opposition, they quickly find out that they are not as good a team as they and everyone else may have thought they were. This can be a devastating shock to a team that has run up a 10–0 record against weak opponents, only to fall flat on their face when they get to conference play. All that confidence can escape like hot air out of a withering balloon, until they are so discouraged they can't recover.

Wiser coaches schedule several very competitive opponents—even some that are a little over their team's head—so that their players are stretched. These adverse situations prepare their teams to meet the more challenging opponents later on in the year.

This correlates to parenting. If you put your kid in an easy math class to give him some confidence, that may be all right for a short period of time, but how will you prepare him to face the more challenging levels? You must also have a "toughening" strategy. We need to make sure that we do not protect our kids from the more challenging issues of life. There comes a time when we need to encourage them to play with the big-ger kid, or let them stand up for themselves rather than protect them

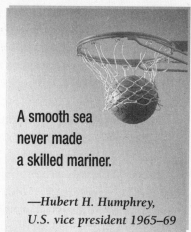

A smooth sea never made a skilled mariner.

—*Hubert H. Humphrey,*
U.S. vice president 1965–69

from the neighborhood bully. There also comes a time when they need to go into situations where they feel a little nervous or shy. You need to encourage them to go forward and do their best even if they don't win.

Don't get me wrong. I'm not speaking here of putting them in moral-ly dangerous situations. I'm talking about encouraging them to face activities, people, and challenges that are difficult—especially as they get older and gain maturity.

Too often kids are not encouraged by their parents to take on chal-lenges if they seem a little nervous or shy. We step in too quickly to pro-tect our kids from any potential embarrassment. When I ran basketball summer camps for younger kids, there were times when I saw great potential in a kid and wanted to put him in with a group of kids who were better than he as a challenge to take him to the next level of play, but then a parent would step in and complain. With the younger or less talented kids he was a star, and his parents liked protecting that image—sometimes for their own gratification—but that was not good for the kid. It didn't stretch him. I wanted to put him in a tougher set-ting but one where, in the long run, he would learn more.

Sometimes, in our effort to protect our kids from adversity, we par-ents shield them from the very thing that would make them better. So, just like a coach scheduling tough teams, welcome a little adversity into the life of your kids. In the end, your kids will be better for it.

Even some of us adults struggle with why life is so tough sometimes. Certainly some of our troubles are the direct consequence of our own foolishness, but one of my favorite verses in the Bible gives this remarkable advice: "Whenever trouble comes your way, let it be an opportunity for joy. For when your faith is tested, your endurance has a chance to grow. So let it grow, for when your endurance is fully developed, you will be strong in character and ready for anything" (James 1:2–4 NLT). Don't deny your kids that experience by overprotection.

Handling the Unexpected

Recently a reorganized Northwestern basketball team under the leadership of my successor, Kevin O'Neill, faced Indiana University. A win for Northwestern would have given them a shot at the postseason NCAA tournament for only the second time in the school's history. Historically Indiana is a powerhouse coached by the highly regarded Bobby Knight, one of the country's most well-known man-to-man defensive coaches. So it was going to be a very challenging game.

Knowing this, Northwestern worked hard on overcoming the man-to-man defense, so hard, in fact, that come game time, they were scoring right and left and Indiana couldn't shut them down. The score was very tight until late in the game when Bobby Knight called a time-out and did the unthinkable: He put his team in a zone defense. Suddenly the tables turned, and Indiana held Northwestern scoreless for seven straight minutes. Now, this is no criticism of the Northwestern team or of Kevin O'Neill, a veteran coach, but the unexpected zone defense caught Northwestern off guard. Who had ever heard of Bobby Knight switching to a zone defense?

But life is like that. We can go along with our game plan, and out of the blue something happens that we were not anticipating. Can we adjust? How we handle those situations often determines whether or not we will be successful in the game of life.

Therefore, an effective game plan for your kids must prepare them for the unexpected. In coaching, I always told my team about the things they were likely to face and I supported those predictions with statistics, reports, anecdotes—whatever would help them take my advice seriously in preparing for what was ahead. But it wasn't so easy to predict or prepare them for the unexpected even though there was a documentable percentage attached it. How do you prepare for something you can't describe and you don't know when, where, why, or how it is going to happen?

I recall listening to a golf program once when the commentator noted that everybody on the golf course was capable of winning. These guys were pros; they all could come off the tee and make great shots. "But," he said, "the one who will win is the one who can play his *bad* shots the best." In other words, if for whatever reason the ball ended up in the sand trap or in the woods, the golfer who could play his way out of the unexpected the best would win. Of course, as pro golfers, these guys weren't expected to hit the ball into sand traps, but what the commentator was pointing out is that *life always includes the unexpected.*

Relax.
God is
still in charge!

In September and October of 1987, playing for the San Francisco Giants, Dave Dravecky pitched the two best games of his entire career. He was riding high, thinking 1988 was going to be his year to win twenty games.

Then he was hit with cancer—to some, the ultimate "unexpected." In 1988 he had surgery to remove 50 percent of his deltoid muscle and a tumor that had developed in his left arm, halfway between the shoulder and the elbow. The doctor said, "Outside of a miracle, you will never pitch again."

But on August 10, 1989, he stood on the mound and threw ninety-three pitches. Before his operation, he had thrown pitches at eighty-eight to ninety miles an hour. In this game he was again clocked at those speeds, even though half of his deltoid muscle and 95 percent of its use was gone.

His miraculous comeback captured the attention of the entire sports world!

However, five days later while pitching against the Montreal Expos, Dravecky hurled a fastball in the sixth inning. The loud crack that accompanied it was not the sound of the bat hitting the ball. It was Dravecky's arm breaking, leaving him writhing in pain out on the mound. The cancer had returned and it ultimately required the amputation of his arm.

His baseball career was over!

In one way, no one can prepare for the unexpected at that magnitude. However, Dravecky's perspective did allow him to make a second comeback of another sort. He believes that God allowed his first miracle in order to provide a national platform for him to share his faith, which he now considers a far more important purpose in life than playing professional baseball.

For Dravecky, preparation for the unexpected first required his coming to faith in God, a God who is good all the time and can be trusted all the time to be good . . . no matter how the circumstances may appear.

As parents trying to develop a game plan for our kids, we too must prepare them for the unexpected. But how? Here are four guidelines I have found helpful.

1. *Help your kids expect the unexpected.* The advent of the unexpected is not the end of the world. For those of us who believe (and even for those who don't), God is still in control. So don't blame life. This *is* life.

2. *Portray the unexpected as an opportunity rather than a disaster.* How you personally respond to the unexpected will have a powerful impact on how your kids respond. What happens when you lose your job? Or when someone runs into the back of your car? Do your kids see you get angry and frustrated? Or do you treat it as an unexpected—maybe even disappointing—event that you deal with evenly?

3. *Tell your kids how other people have met unexpected challenges and gotten through them.* This dynamic characterizes every true hero. This is the power of stories—classic stories, stories about true sports heroes, stories about your parents, stories from your own experience.

4. *Remind them to stick to the fundamentals of their game plan and not to panic.* Stay steady, and they will come through.

As I mentioned earlier, before our kids went to school, we prepared them for the fact that someone would probably pick out something unique about them and tease them for it. When other kids tease my kids, I believe they are able to roll with the punches a little bit better than if we had led them to believe that life was going to roll out before them like a red carpet. We can't predict *what* they will encounter, but we have taught them to expect the unexpected because we know that the world is not populated only by Mr. Nice Guys.

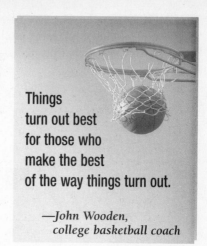

Things turn out best for those who make the best of the way things turn out.

—*John Wooden,
college basketball coach*

INSTANT REPLAY

Ben Carson, the highly acclaimed African-American neurosurgeon, went from a "total failure" in the fifth grade to receive a full scholarship to Yale, after his mother put together a new game plan: shut off the TV and read books! You might say, "We couldn't possibly do something so radical." And I'm not saying you should. I'm not even saying academic performance is the most important priority in your child's game plan. However, when you discover what your child needs—whether it has to do with school, friends, faith, controlling media input, or dealing with the unexpected—don't say it's impossible.

Ben Carson offers this poignant illustration for dealing with "the impossible."

> Suppose you were to walk up to a panhandler on the sidewalk in downtown Baltimore. He has been telling everyone that he is out of work and needs money just to buy supper. You promise him if he can get to Bismarck, North Dakota, within twenty-four hours, a very nice job will be waiting for him there. What happens? Chances are he will look at you as though you are crazy and inform you he has no way of getting to Bismarck. . . .
>
> Now just suppose that, instead of a job offer, you could absolutely guarantee that same panhandler $1 million if he would meet you in Bismarck, North Dakota, within twenty-four hours. What do you think would happen?[5]

---

[5]Ben Carson with Gregg Lewis, *The Big Picture* (Grand Rapids, Mich.: Zondervan Publishing House, 1999), 125–26.

Carson's point is obvious. We can do far more than we ever imagined if we make our game plan a high enough priority. You may be surprised when your child makes it "to Bismarck," right on time.

FREE THROW

1. On a scale of one to five, with one being weak and five being strong, how would you evaluate the four areas of offense in your game plan for your children?
   - education
   - extracurricular activities
   - friendships
   - a solid faith

2. On a scale of one to five, how would you evaluate the effectiveness of your defensive game plan in the following areas?
   - negative peers
   - television
   - music
   - idle time

3. On a scale of one to five, how do *you* deal with the unexpected?
   - Do you expect the unexpected?
   - Do you consider the unexpected an opportunity (rather than a disaster)?
   - When faced with the unexpected, are you able to focus on the fundamentals of your game plan without panicking?

4. In each of the previous three categories, select the item in which you scored the lowest and write a brief commitment for how you intend to improve in that area.

5. Recall three stories that you might share with your children about how other people have met unexpected challenges and gotten through them.

7. HOME COURT ADVANTAGE

The first time I saw Cobo Arena in downtown Detroit, I scratched my head and raised a disbelieving eyebrow. "We're going to play basketball on top of an *ice rink*?"

I had just signed on as head basketball coach at the University of Detroit Mercy and was taking a look at our "home court," which, I learned, we shared with a hockey team. My dismay wasn't entirely unfounded. We discovered early on during practices that there was a tremendous amount of condensation on the court because of the ice rink beneath the floor. But we also discovered that certain spots were more slippery than others, and after practicing on the floor numerous times, it became almost second nature to play around them. Soon the team was able to play with a lot of freedom and confidence in the Cobo Arena, simply based on knowing where the danger spots were.

Not that we bothered to share that information with our opponents.

Our opponents did not have this comfort level when they came to play Detroit. The visiting team knew an ice rink lay beneath the basketball court, but not knowing where condensation collected on the floor gave them one or two more things to think about during a game, and they had to play with a certain level of caution. This meant, of course, that we had an additional advantage when we played our home games at Cobo Arena.

Not many basketball courts are built on top of an ice rink, but Cobo Arena is not alone in providing an advantage to its home team. Coaches, players, and sports broadcasters are always talking about "home court advantage"—the number of games a team tends to win on its home court versus the number it wins on the road.

NBA teams play an eighty-two-game season, and the teams are highly motivated to gain a home court advantage for the playoffs. Why? After the first round, the playoffs have seven games. The team that has the best regular season record will end up playing *four* games on their home court and *three* games on the opponent's court. Each team works hard to obtain that home court advantage because the statistics are overwhelming: *Teams win more games on their home floor*. Some advantage comes from familiarity with physical characteristics—the floor, the lighting, the air conditioning—but much of it comes from the fans.

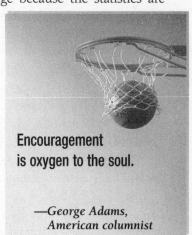

Encouragement is oxygen to the soul.

—*George Adams, American columnist*

Many coaches will only take jobs where the home community has shown a great interest in the basketball team. Their encouragement is invaluable. Coaches know that if there is a strong interest in the team, they'll have the opportunity to build a tremendous home court advantage. When I was an assistant coach at the University of Arizona, we had one of the most phenomenal home court advantages in college basketball. We didn't lose a home game in the 1985–86 and the 1987–88 seasons. This phenomenon continued in 1988–89, the year after I left.

Now, we all knew it was an advantage to play on our home court. But I was curious: exactly *why* was it an advantage? So, like a dedicated gossip columnist ("inquiring minds want to know"), I asked my players why they thought they won most of their games at home.

FAMILIARITY BREEDS CONFIDENCE

First thing out of their mouths: "We're *familiar with our surroundings*." They knew the court, they knew the lay of the land in the arena, they knew the people who were cooking their food and cleaning the locker rooms, they were able to sleep in their own beds at night prior to the game. They didn't have to think about a lot of peripheral things because they were already familiar with how those things operated. They could relax and focus their attention on what was most important: the game. The home court gave them confidence to face even a tough opponent.

But when you are the road team, the arena is unfamiliar; the faces in the stands are strange; the food, the beds, the transportation are all different. Even though one seldom realizes it, an enormous amount of energy and attention goes toward coping with an unfamiliar environment. It's harder to relax and concentrate on the game at hand. Even if you figure out the particular challenges of an unfamiliar court, it's just one more thing to have to think about; it's not second nature; you're out of your comfort zone. So each game has a whole set of new challenges, and the road team feels as though it's going through the struggle alone.

Curious, isn't it? The same thing is true for the kids God gave you to raise. As the family coach, you need to realize that whenever your kids are outside the home they are competing on unfamiliar territory. They're "on the road," so to speak. You might not think of the school, the playground, friends' homes, or the neighborhood as competition. But don't be fooled, these *are* areas of competition to your kids.

How many hours a day do your children spend outside of the home trying to be accepted by their classmates and friends, figuring out the pecking order on the playground, anxious about whether they'll be chosen for the baseball team, and just how safe they feel in their neighborhood? Even at school, they have to figure out which teachers are approachable, how social groups fall out in the lunchroom (a stratified society if there ever was one), and schoolwork they don't quite understand. All of these things are challenges that our kids face outside of the home.

So when our children come home, they need that sense of safety and security associated with the familiar. They shouldn't have to wonder if anyone is going to be home or if someone is going to fix dinner. At home they should be able to relax and find comfort as they figure out how to navigate the life issues that face them "out there." Just as my players in Detroit felt safe on the home court because they knew where the slippery spots were, our kids need to feel safe at home in order to deal with the challenges they are facing away from home.

But for a "home court" to build that kind of confidence, we as parents must provide an environment that is *consistent*. I've already mentioned that when I had my team on our own turf, we set a specific practice time each day, ate together at a particular time, and even imposed a curfew to help the team be ready for the next game. Our routine got disrupted when we played on the road, and that sometimes put us off our rhythm. But once we got home, we got back into our own routine, and the players were able to relax and rebuild their confidence.

If you want to provide your kids with confidence to handle the challenges they face in the game of life, your home must operate with a certain level of consistency and order. Kids can't produce quality homework when the television is on constantly. Kids who stay up till all hours won't be rested and alert at school the next day. Teens who skip meals or eat out of the refrigerator can't do their best work or play. Kids whose parents are rarely home live with a certain amount of anxiety—is there somebody there for me?—which diminishes their capacity to function.

Coaches who want their team to win know the players need rest and would consider it absurd to put the players next door to someone who was playing loud music or partying all night. (Some coaches move their teams to a hotel before an important game, even in their hometown, to assure control of the environment.) I am sometimes surprised at the things coaches do in order to give their players the best opportunity to succeed, but it is even more surprising how little attention some parents pay to consistency, order, proper food and rest, and a regular schedule at home. The fact is, we parents should be *more* diligent than the coach of a sports team to give our kids a chance to win an even more important game—the game of life.

A SENSE OF FAIR PLAY

The second thing that gives a team a sense of confidence when playing on their home court is their belief that they'll be treated fairly. When we were playing on the road, sometimes my players expressed concern over certain calls by the officials that tended to favor the other team. I won't say officials went out of their way to make "bad" calls. However, I can say that *believing* they got a fairer shake from the guys in stripes on their home court boosted my players' confidence when we played home games.

Why is this? On the road, playing in a strange town with a lot of unfamiliar faces in the stands, a team tends to feel alone and unsupported. No one cares much if a call goes against them. But when a team is competing at home, they know the pressure is on for refs to be scrupulously fair because a lot of people in the stands have a vested interest in the contest. When we played a home game at Northwestern University, there were eight thousand people in the arena who wanted to see Northwestern win that game. The fans wouldn't tolerate unfair officiating, and their boisterous disapproval of sloppy calls kept the officials focused on doing a good job.

Good officials don't go into games looking to make unfair calls, but when there are people in the crowd rooting for your success, it encourages the officials to at least give their best effort on your behalf. The home team may get several favorable calls that might have been passed over if they were playing in a setting where no one seemed to care whether they won the game or not. In fact, most fans and players have observed instances when an official has accidentally made a wrong call that fans object to loudly. Without retracting the call, an official will sometimes compensate with a call that "leans" the other way, not a counterbalancing "wrong" call, but one where judgment could take it either way.

This basic concept is true in other areas of life as well. Our criminal justice system tries to make sure that people are tried by a jury of their peers, based on the belief that the accused will get the fairest hearing from people who are generally like them. This environment provides a person with the best chance of being fairly judged.

What does this say about our kids and their "home court"? There are a lot of ways that life isn't fair. They need to accept that, but our sons and daughters also need the confidence that there's at least one "playing field" where they will always get a fair shake. When my kids feel like they're being mistreated at school or with their friends, the first place they come to explain what happened is home, because they know Mom and Dad have their best interests at heart.

I'm not talking about bending the rules or putting on the attitude that "my kid couldn't possibly be in the wrong." But at least our kids know that their mother and I want them to be winners at life, so they can count on us to help them work things out fairly. This actually gives them the internal confidence they need to handle situations *outside* the home that don't seem fair.

In one of our local middle schools, a young man I know walked into class late one day and, being a bit of a clown, struck a pose as if to say, "Here I am!" Annoyed at the disruption, the teacher grabbed him by the shirt and slammed the boy against the wall. The boy was badly shaken and felt he had been treated unfairly.

To his parents, the boy admitted he had been wrong to come in late and disrupt the class. "But, Dad," he said, "all the teacher had to do was say something, and I would have sat down. Or given me a detention. But he shouldn't have gotten physical." His parents agreed—both that their son had been wrong and that the teacher had overreacted. The parents did *not* charge into the school demanding the removal of the teacher. In fact, the parents did nothing. But they did support their son in his decision to ask the principal for a meeting with the teacher—a calm discussion that cleared the air.

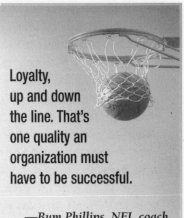

Loyalty, up and down the line. That's one quality an organization must have to be successful.

—*Bum Phillips, NFL coach*

What if things hadn't worked out at school? The boy would still know he got a fair hearing at home, giving him confidence that he could discern a situation, own up to his responsibility, but also sort out what seemed unfair.

In sports, nothing discourages a player more than believing that the game is being played unfairly. Why even try? It's true at school; it's true in the workplace. If you go to work each day, doing the same job as the person next to you, maybe even more, and for whatever reason that particular person gets a promotion or a raise—how do you feel? Suppose it not only happens once but again and again. You'd start to feel discouraged and probably lose your motivation to excel in that particular corporation.

The same is true with your kids as they try to win in the game of life. If they sense the odds are stacked against them—the school is pushing them into a vocational track when they'd like to go to college, or nobody will hire them for an after-school job, or girls aren't allowed to try out for track—it's easy to lose motivation to try. This doesn't mean we should fight their battles for them or even let them turn everything into a "pity party." But it is important that we parents provide one area where they have confidence that we're giving them a fair chance to succeed—on their own "home court."

FAN SUPPORT

A third—and maybe the most important—reason why there's an advantage to playing on the home court is because the team is surrounded by a group of cheering, adoring fans. Besides the fact that we'd all rather be cheered than jeered, I'd like to look at a number of reasons why fan support is so critical.

Fans cheer for their team before the contest has even started. Fans come to the arena with a tremendous amount of anticipation about the game, and the minute their team runs onto the floor for warm-up, they begin cheering. Note that the team hasn't proved anything yet. The fans are cheering prior to the contest's start! The players know before the game begins that they have support. Someone will be with them in this battle. No player likes playing in front of a group of people that want to see how they will perform before they will be accepted. That's why acceptance on the home court is so important. It takes place prior to the contest.

Plain and simple, our kids need to know that Mom and Dad are their biggest fans without their having to "do" something to win our approval. They need to know *we* think they're going to be winners. Imagine the support your kids would feel if each day when they come home, they knew you were eagerly awaiting their arrival, just as fans sit in the stands prior to the game waiting for their team to run out onto the floor.

Kids need to know that Mom and Dad are their biggest fans!

Please, if I can encourage you to do anything, show that type of enthusiasm for your kids when they arrive home each day from the rigors of life as kids know it—whatever that is. A kid's challenge may be just holding his or her own on the playground, so let's just assume that when they hit your front door, they need to be cheered and welcomed by you.

Obviously your kids would look at you funny if you clapped and whistled and yelled like a sports fan when they walked in the door, but your "cheer" might be a smile and a welcome-home hug or "Hey! I'm glad to see you." The bottom line, though, is that it needs to be consistent. I have never been at a sports contest yet where the fans did not cheer when the home team ran out. So every day when your kids wake up or when they come home from school, they need to be greeted with a certain real "cheer."

Fans support you when you play well or score. OK, the game begins and a player on the home team makes a good play. The cheering now is even louder than when the players ran out onto the floor. And if that play results in a score or the winning point, the fans are out of their seats.

How do we respond when our kids do something positive? We need to cheer even louder. If they come home with a report card with grades that have improved over last time, cheer louder. (Don't wait till it's all A's.) Most of us parents find this pretty easy to do when our kids "score points"—when they make the honor roll, win a part in the school play, or are chosen team captain. But there are lots of smaller things we should cheer for too: Trisha remembers to take out the trash; Trevor reads to his little sister while you're on the phone; Tiffany cheerfully gives up her bed when Grandma comes to visit. Don't take these things for granted. Kids need encouragement and reinforcement when they do well.

Parents, take note: if we *only* cheer when our kids make the big "score," our cheers can create anxiety instead of confidence. Are Mom and Dad only rooting for me if I win? Will I be good enough? How high do I have to jump before they cheer? That's why it's important to let our kids know that we're rooting for them to begin with, just because they're the "home team."

Fans support you when you make mistakes. On the home court, my players felt that *they could make mistakes and still be accepted.* In every game there are going to be a number of mistakes before that game is over. But one great thing about playing at home is that the crowd doesn't feed on your mistakes.

The opposite is usually true when you play on the road. The crowd often heckles you, ridicules you, and calls you all kinds of names for making a mistake. How many times in a basketball game have you seen a player on the visiting team shoot an air ball, and every time he gets the ball in his hands after that, the crowd yells, "Air ball! Air ball!"? People don't forget; in fact, they like to hold that mistake over your

head and keep you thinking about it. They rub it in and make it difficult for you to live it down.

On the home court, however, that is not going to happen. If a home
boy shoots an air ball, the fans are not going to constantly remind him

 of it. In fact, they're already on to the
next play, encouraging him, letting him
know he can do it.

Parents, ask yourselves: Do your kids
know they can make a mistake and they
won't be ridiculed for it? Do they know
Mom and Dad aren't going to hold it
over their heads, bringing it up again
and again, rubbing it in? Are you ready
to let them move on to the next thing,
giving them encouragement that you
know they can do it?

If we only cheer when our kids make the big "score," our cheers can create anxiety instead of confidence.

Recently Ricky Jr.'s teacher called and
said that he was not behaving the way he should in class. Obviously
this was disappointing news to Sherialyn and me. No parent wants to
find out that his son or daughter is behaving in a way that distracts from
the learning that should take place in a classroom.

We let Ricky know we were concerned and wanted to stay on top of
what was going on. So we asked the teacher to give us a day-to-day
evaluation of his behavior—good, bad, fantastic—and she sent home a
note on a daily basis. When we got the note, we discussed with Ricky
what she considered to be bad behavior and why she considered his
behavior unacceptable.

Now, I had told Ricky that if his reports came back more consistently
on a negative side, that he would lose some of his privileges—watching
TV or playing with his PlayStation, things we knew he enjoyed. In
addressing the situation, we put in some measures that we thought
would help turn that behavior around. *But how could we cheer him during the process?* How could we encourage him as his biggest fans? I did-
n't enjoy taking away his fun. I knew he was basically a good kid and
could do better. So in the morning when he was getting ready to go to
school, I'd say, "Hey, good luck today. I'm pulling for you. I hope the
teacher thinks your behavior is acceptable so that you can do the things
that you want to do." And when he came back with a good report, we
said, "We knew you could do it."

Fans support you when the team is down. I think most coaches would agree with me that the fans are *most* important when the team is down. A home court advantage doesn't mean the home team always wins. Sometimes a team playing at home will fall into a slump and get behind, and it will be the cheering and encouragement from the crowd that gives the players a shot of adrenaline, newfound energy that comes from the energy they feel in the crowd. The crowd noise and enthusi-

We add yesterday's successes to today's lessons to create tomorrow's victories.

—*Ken Ruettgers,*
NFL offensive tackle

asm tends to lift the players to a new level of confidence, and they are able to use that energy to overcome whatever deficit they find themselves in.

The support of true-blue fans is unconditional. They cheer when the team is ahead, and they cheer when the team is behind, but it is this cheering when the team is behind that is most significant and most difficult to do. Of course it's easy to cheer for a team that is playing well, scoring baskets, making touchdowns, hitting home runs. But the team that finds itself behind by twenty points in a basketball game—that's the team that needs to hear from the fans the most. Sports teams that win games on a consistent basis at home have fans that understand the importance of cheering when the team is down.

Now, admittedly, at home this is often the most difficult area of support. Most parents are excited when their kids do well, but are you cheering for your kids when things *don't* go so well? I'm not talking about mistakes like breaking a china plate or forgetting to put gas in the car so that you run out on the way to work. What has been your reaction when your kids have done things that put them *behind in life?* Their grades have fallen and they've started hanging out with friends you don't think are desirable. Or maybe it's something even more serious. You discover that your teenager has been experimenting with drugs or alcohol. Or your high schooler, for whom you had so many high hopes and dreams, has suddenly become a parent in the ninth or tenth grade.

These are important issues and should concern you a great deal. But all these things represent kids being down in life. Even as you demonstrate your concern and seek out the appropriate methods to turn these events around, the question still has to be asked: How can I continue to encourage and cheer my kids on to success? Sports fans keep cheering for their home team even when they are on a losing streak. Shouldn't we parents do this for our kids when they fall behind in life? After all, a basketball season is just a basketball season. But for our kids, the stakes are much higher; this is the game of *life*.

Kids who are falling behind in life need to hear that you still believe in them, that you're still their number one fan. Does that mean we condone their poor choices or wrong actions? No. But our words and attitudes and actions can tell our kids that we believe that they can come back, and that we are going to keep cheering even as they work on what they need to do to get their lives back on track. After all, the New Testament tells the story of Jesus confronting a woman who had been caught cheating on her husband. What did He say to her? "Go, and sin no more" (see John 8 in the Bible). He didn't browbeat her; He didn't condone her behavior either. What He did do is stick up for her in the presence of a jeering crowd and tell her that her life didn't have to go this way; she could turn her life around.

But, you might be asking, how do you cheer for a kid who is going down the wrong road? I know there are no simple answers when a kid seems to be doing everything wrong, but no matter what the score is, *the game goes on.* Even if a team is down, the game still needs to be played, and it isn't going to help anything if the fans quit cheering. The same is true with our kids. The game of life goes on, and as long as the game is playing, it's always helpful to encourage them in their situation. No, we don't ignore things that have happened; yes, we try to put things in order to prevent destructive behavior from continuing. Cheering for them doesn't mean we are cheering for what they are doing if it is wrong, but never lose sight of how important it is to cheer for our kids when they are down.

Are you a fair-weather fan? Even though we've been talking about the importance of fan support in giving a team a home court advantage, not everyone in the home crowd is as supportive as they should be. Probably the most hurtful experience an athlete can experi-

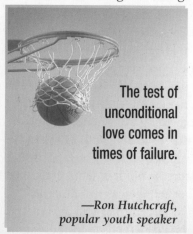

The test of unconditional love comes in times of failure.

—*Ron Hutchcraft, popular youth speaker*

ence is being booed by the home fans, but it happens. It makes you appreciate even more those fans who—even in the midst of a booing crowd—are supportive through thick and thin.

Fair-weather fans in the stands are no fun, but dealing with them is part of being an athlete. Parents, listen up: *We cannot afford to be fair-weather fans in the home*. The fans in the stands talk about "their team" and rehash player stats and plays as if they knew each athlete personally, but those fans do not have the intimate bond and influential relationship with the players that parents have with their kids. Parents rank at the top of the list of people whose support—or lack of it—matters to kids.[1]

Parents who are fair-weather fans are more akin to a coach who has nothing good to say to his players unless they score big points. This "conditional support" can be extremely hurtful to a kid.

When I went to Northwestern University as head coach, we had a great first season and went all the way to the postseason tournament—something that team had achieved only one other time in the history of the school. But following that season, our team fell on hard times. Injuries and a number of other factors made it difficult to sustain the success we had achieved. The fans got restless and attendance at games started to drop off.

Now, I don't blame the fans. I know that's part of sports, so I anticipated some drop-off. But it was tough. At the same time, I'll never forget the core of people sitting behind my bench who *always* applauded when I came out onto the court and *always* applauded as I left, through thick and thin. Even after a loss, they stood and cheered the effort of the team. "Keep your head up, Coach!" they'd say. "It'll be better next time!" The unconditional support of those boosters helped make my experience at Northwestern rewarding even though as a basketball team we had some difficult times with our win/loss record.

Now, when we played on the opposition's court, those die-hard fans were replaced by a group of hecklers who rubbed it in each time our team performed below par.

In the game of life, our kids will have more than their share of

---

[1] John W. Welte, William F. Wieczorek, and Lenning Zhang, "Peer and Parental Influences on Male Adolescent Drinking," in *Research in Brief* (May 1998), Research Institute on Addictions. www.ria.org. While it is tempting to think that by the age of 16–19 parents don't count and peers are all that matters, this study shows that parents still do influence their kids. Specifically, "parental alcohol-related attitudes are more important than parental drinking in accounting for adolescent drinking, while peer drinking is more critical than peer alcohol-related attitudes."

naysayers, ready to pounce on every mistake or weakness. So never lose sight of how important it is, when things aren't going well for your kids, to have *someone* cheering them on and keeping them going until things get better.

In your family, that someone needs to be *you*.

In real life, not every parent is as supportive as they should be. But I've heard many kids in single parent homes testify, "Dad ran out on us, but Mom was always there for me. She believed I could do it." Or maybe it's Grandma or Granddad, or an older brother or sister who remained a consistent cheerleader on their behalf. Whatever relationship you have to the kids in your life, be the cheerleader they need through thick and thin.

THE FAMILY "LOCKER ROOM"
(TAKING YOUR HOME COURT ADVANTAGE WITH YOU)

Even on the road, each team has its own locker room. The locker room is where the players can let down their guard, be themselves, just the team together. All the "in" jokes come out in the locker room, the team banter that is part of the team identity. The coach can choose whether or not to let in the press or other folks. Sometimes the coach and the team just need to be alone, to get that pep talk, to put what happened out on the floor into perspective, to be reminded of "who we are" even in a strange environment. The hecklers are shut out for a few moments. It's a time to get one's bearings.

Before the game, the locker room is where the coach reminds the team what they're all about and tells them to keep focused on the game, not to be distracted by the antics of the other team's mascot or the unfamiliar court. *At half time*, the locker room is where the team can regroup, look at their game plan, see if their strategy is advancing their goal. *After the game*, the locker room is where the team celebrates its victory or deals with the disappointment of defeat in a way that enables them to say, "Next time!"

In a sense, the locker room—even on the road—is an oasis where the team can tap into some of its "home court advantage."

What kinds of things make up *your* family's "locker room"?

The family locker room is made up of all the family traditions and values, big and small, that say, "This is *our* family! This is who we are! This is what we stand for!" It's wearing matching T-shirts to the company picnic; always serving chocolate cake at breakfast on birthdays;

passing on a family name generation after generation; taking the phone off the hook on family nights; going to church together; turning the burned Thanksgiving dinner disaster into family "folklore"; making up a funny song to sing at Grandma and Grandpa's fiftieth anniversary party; taking your son or daughter camping, just the two of you; or working on your family mission statement.

Your family traditions, values, and memories all become part of each child's identity—the identity they take with them, whether it's off to junior high for a long school day or moving away from home for the first time.

A friend of mine tells how homesick she was when she first went away to college, two thousand miles from home, for the first time. Because of the distance, she was lucky if she went home for Christmas—and *forget* Thanksgiving or spring break. Her parents wrote regularly, but it just wasn't the same as talking at the dinner table or having Mom say, "How was your day?"

"When I was feeling really down," she says, "I'd remember how it was as a child waking up in the early morning to go to the bathroom and seeing my dad on his knees in the living room praying out loud. I'd pause by the doorway and eavesdrop, and I'd hear him pray for each one of us kids by name. Even when my older sister and brother went away to college, I'd hear him pray for them. So I knew *that very day*, my dad had been up at the crack of dawn praying for *me*. It was a tremendous source of strength to me and gave me the courage to go on."

That's the family locker room at work, providing a home court advantage whether the game is on your turf or on the road.

INSTANT REPLAY

Obviously I think giving our kids a home court advantage is critical to the success of the family team. But that doesn't mean I want my kids to be afraid to go on the road. The home court is not the only place they must win.

In 1986 the film *Hoosiers* brought us the story of a high school basketball coach who molded the raw talent from Hickory, Indiana, into a winning team that went all the way to the state finals.[2]

As the team of "country boys" walked into the enormous arena where they would face Butler High School, their jaws dropped. Every

---

[2]*Hoosiers*, starring Gene Hackman, is rated PG and is available from your video store.

one of them seemed to shrink, like lone grasshoppers in a cornfield. The first thing Coach Norman Dale (Gene Hackman) did was ask one of his players to measure the distance from the line behind the basket to the free-throw line.

"Fifteen feet," said his player.

Next the coach asked his shortest player to climb on the shoulders of the tallest player and measure the distance from the basketball rim to the floor.

The measuring tape spun out. "Ten feet."

The coach looked at his players and grinned. "Just like home."

It was a defining moment. The colors painted on the floor, the number of seats in the arena, the acoustics—all might vary from place to place. But the game hadn't changed. They had practiced on a court *just like this one*. Without even saying the words, the coach was cheering his team on: "You can do it. You can do it *here*!"

We need to be that kind of coach for our kids. Give them a home court advantage, and let them take it on the road.

FREE THROW

1. Evaluate your home court advantage by rating your consistency in the following areas.

	Never		**Always**
I provide a quiet environment for my kids to study in.	1	3	5
I see that my kids get plenty of rest in order to be fit for school each day.	1	3	5
I make sure that my kids eat balanced, nutritious meals.	1	3	5
My family sits down to eat together at least five times a week.	1	3	5
My kids know where I am and how to contact me if they need me.	1	3	5
At least one parent is at home to greet my kids when they get home.	1	3	5
I make time for my kids to talk to me, and I listen.	1	3	5

2. In the average week there are 112 waking hours (for those who sleep eight hours per night). Estimate the amount of time each week that your children spend "on the road," that is, time when they are not at home enjoying their home court advantage. Include daycare, school, going to and from school (unless you take them), playing at a friend's house, spending time "hanging out," time at church, taking lessons, playing sports, or doing anything else away from home or without your direct supervision. This is not to question the value of these activities. It is only to emphasize the importance of enhancing the stability and consistency of your home court advantage when your kids are home. Make separate calculations for each child.

3. Briefly describe an instance when you supported your child even though he or she made a mistake or was "losing." Be sure to note *how* you expressed your support.

4. Describe a situation when you acted more like a fair-weather fan. How do you wish you had responded? Be specific in thinking of something you could have said or done. Even now, is there some way you should rectify this situation?

8. RULES OF THE GAME

It made for good TV. No question.

The Chicago Bulls were going hard against the Minnesota Timberwolves in Minneapolis on January 15, 1997, when the flamboyant Dennis Rodman missed a rebound and chased it off the court. No sooner had he crossed the black line than he tripped over a photographer and fell across a TV cameraman. The next moment, the TV guy was doubled up in pain. Frustrated and angry that the cameraman was in his way, Rodman had kicked him in the groin. (Ouch!)

NBA officials reacted immediately, dishing out an eleven-game suspension and a $25,000 fine to the controversial superstar. The media was all over the story for the next few weeks. The punishment was too tough . . . not tough enough. . . . Rodman should be given the boot permanently. . . . How long do we have to suffer his antics? . . . All right, he got carried away, but he's the rebound king.

Like I said, it made for good TV, good copy.

Most people—and that includes basketball players—do not like being penalized for their actions. So it's no wonder that any "disciplinary action" often stirs up confrontation and controversy. And not just by the media. Whenever the issue was discipline on our college teams, the phone would start ringing—calls from parents, friends, or anyone else with a personal interest in the player, all offering their two cents worth.

But I think that narrowly defining discipline as "punishment" is part of the problem. In this chapter, I'd like to focus on a broader view of discipline, one in which punishment—or the consequences of our actions—is not only put into a larger context but is actually only a small part of the discipline process. When this happens, consequences are not only more effective but you are also more likely to get a favorable response from the individual who is being disciplined.

DISCIPLINE AS DISCIPLESHIP

Look at those two words. Notice how much the word *discipline* looks like the word *disciple*. They both come from the same Latin root, meaning "pupil" or "instruction." Disciple is not a word one normally associates with punishment. In fact, we usually associate it with teaching or training, showing someone the way.

When I hear the word *disciple*, I personally think of the motley crew that made up Jesus' Twelve. They included blue-collar fishermen, a government agent (with about as much popularity as the IRS), a political activist, married guys, single guys—a pretty diverse bunch. They were called "disciples" because they chose to follow Christ and to learn from His teachings. But they weren't saints. They argued among themselves, jockeyed for position, got angry with their critics, and were better at bragging than doing. Once Jesus even had to say, in effect, to Simon Peter, "Shut up!" (See Matthew 6:23 in the Bible.) But Jesus spent three years teaching the disciples, training them, preparing them, sharing His wisdom, so that they could carry on when He was no longer with them.

His "discipline" or "discipling" paid off. When Jesus had accomplished His ministry, this ordinary bunch of men spread Christ's message throughout the known world, and were so strong in their convictions that most of them paid for it with their lives.

Both as a coach and as a parent, it helps me to understand that the concept of discipline and discipling are both in the same family. Understanding the relationship puts discipline in a much more positive context, with punishment or "consequences for misbehavior" just one aspect of a well-balanced training and development program.

If we think of discipline as training, it's easy to understand why discipline is necessary to the success of any high school, college, or professional ball team. Bobby Knight, Hall of Fame coach at Indiana University, had a definition for discipline that a lot of coaches like: "Do what you are supposed to do, when you are supposed to do it, how you are supposed to do it, and do it that way every time." That's a hefty goal!

Nevertheless, that's exactly what each coach wants for his team.

We've all seen coaches on TV ranting and raving up and down the sidelines, trying to get their teams to "do what they're supposed to do, when they're supposed to do it, how they're supposed do it . . . every time." Sometimes people corner me and ask, "Byrdsong! Why do players take that in-your-face stuff from the coach?"

> The role of discipline is not to impose our will on our children but to help them develop the ability to make right choices as well as the desire to make them.
>
> —*Larry Richards, author*

Good question! (Obviously certain things are more accepted in athletics than they would be in a family.) But the answer is the key to developing a well-rounded approach to discipline.

RELATIONSHIP BEFORE RULES

The reason coaches can dish out that kind of discipline is because *they have a good relationship with their players*. The best coaches establish a solid bond with their team, so that when the pressure is on and the coach says, "Do it this way and do it now!" the players know where the coach is coming from.

They know—get this—that the coach loves them.

By the time sports fans see a team run out onto the court at the start of the season, months have already gone into their training. And in those months, a strong relationship has developed between coach and players. All the TV cameras see is a coach ranting and raving on the sidelines, but the players know this person as someone who cares about them and has their best interests at heart.

Each year prior to the start of official basketball practice, my staff and I got the whole team together and played . . . softball! That's right. We divided up the players and staff into two teams and just had a lot of fun. We also scheduled a couple of barbecues with a few other friends of the team. By the time we reached the basketball floor and got down to the rigors of training, we had already laughed a lot and had stories to tell about who charred the burgers or who fell down running from first base to second. (The players *especially* got a kick out of striking out the head coach!)

These activities always worked well to help us develop a relationship outside of the coach/player context. The recruits had grown up watching college ball on TV, just like the fans, and all they'd seen of the coaches were those strict guys in suits on the sidelines, giving the players "what for." So for players to see the coaches in a different context

A relationship is like a bank; you can't draw anything out until you put something in.

and have a chance to experience us as real people brought a different level of trust and closeness to the group.

I also felt it was important to invite the players into my home. This not only gave them a chance to get away from the campus and away from the gym but it also gave them an opportunity to watch their coach interact with his own family. They saw how I treated my wife, and when they heard me talk with my three kids, they understood they weren't the only ones being challenged to be their best. By the time the season started, Ricky, Kelley, Sabrina, and the team were on a first-name basis, and my kids had picked up fifteen new brothers.

When a coach has established a good relationship with his or her players, it is rare to see players rebelling against tough discipline. My experience both on and off the court is that people will do a good many hard things if they believe there are tremendous benefits in store for them, and they will accept challenges from people they believe really care about them and have their best interests at heart.

A slogan I reminded myself of a lot while coaching was, "Rules without relationship equals rebellion." This is true in coaching, but it's especially true in parenting. We can get by "enforcing the rules" for a while, but if we truly want to discipline our children in the sense of training and instructing them so they understand that the rules are for their benefit, it all needs to happen in the context of a strong, loving relationship.

Yet with today's hectic pace and demands on our time, actually spending time with our children doesn't happen automatically. Many families consider themselves lucky if they eat a meal together once a week! We must be very *intentional* about establishing and maintaining a close relationship with our children if we want them to accept our discipline and not rebel against it.

I've already mentioned that I spend a lot of time at the park playing with my kids. Having fun together is an important aspect of our relationship. And I don't *send* my kids to church; I *take* them. If I think an active faith is important for our family, then we need to worship together. I also try to make sure that my kids come to my job occasionally and meet the people I work with so they can see me in that context. I don't want what I do to be a big mystery. I want to be involved in their lives, and I want to involve them in mine.

I don't want to be the kind of parent who only shows up in his kid's life when there's a problem and then hands down punishment. I want to be by their side on a constant basis so that a trusting relationship is forged, and when I have to be the "bad guy" enforcing the rules, they trust me that what I do is for their own good.

Before I move on, I want to make one thing clear: I am not recommending that parents deal with their kids in the aggressive, in-your-face style you see in athletics. This is an accepted way of "doing business" in the world of competitive sports. I used it as an example only to show just what level of tough discipline a person will take *if* a good relationship has been established and the player knows that the coach has his best interest at heart. Hopefully, in parenting situations, we should not have to go to that level in dealing with our children. But the bottom line is: No positive disciplining can take place if it is not happening in the context of a good relationship.

SETTING CLEAR EXPECTATIONS

Part of a solid relationship is clear communication.

A friend of mine told me about Jim, a hospital chaplain in the Chicago area, father of three grown children, and a grandfather. While driving with his wife and some out-of-town friends, Jim made a right turn off a main artery onto a side street. Moments later blue lights were flashing in his rearview mirror, and one of Chicago's finest pulled him over. His infraction? He had made a right turn in front of a bus.

"What bus?" asked Jim incredulously. No one in the car had seen a bus.

The officer informed Jim that, indeed, a bus had been traveling half a block behind him. And there's a law in Chicago that says: "No right turn in front of a bus." Jim's car was "in front of" the bus, and he made a right turn. Ergo, he had made a right turn in front of a bus. A sev-

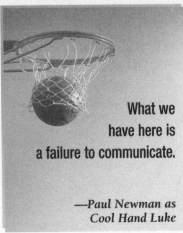

**What we
have here is
a failure to communicate.**

*—Paul Newman as
Cool Hand Luke*

enty-five dollar ticket was issued.

Everyone who hears this story howls, "You've got to be kidding! That law is supposed to prevent drivers from cutting around a stopped bus and making a right turn in front of it!"

You can relate, right? Somewhere, sometime you've had a schoolteacher or a coach or an employer or a foreman who acted as though you ought to know what the rules are, when in reality you only discovered the interpretation of those rules when you stepped over an invisible line and ended up in trouble. Sometimes the rule is stated clearly enough, but *your* interpretation doesn't always go over so good.

Unfortunately a lot of parents operate like that. We tell our kids vaguely to "be good" and wonder why they jump on the bed or use the plastic laundry basket to slide down the carpeted stairs.

Our coaching staff always made it a point to tell the team up front what the rules were and what the penalties would be for any infractions. Skipping class, being late to practice, disrespecting the coach, using alcohol or drugs—each player knew the rules and what would happen if he chose to ignore them. Clear communication was key.

But I remember violating this principle with my own son, Ricky, when he was about six.

Ricky was the type of kid you could send for a glass of water and an hour later have to go looking for him. He'd be somewhere playing baseball, having totally forgotten that you'd asked for a glass of water. His mom and I were getting pretty frustrated with his inability to complete a task without getting sidetracked. Not only that, but his teachers were starting to pick up on the same thing at school. At teacher/parent conferences, we were told that he was not successfully completing his work. He couldn't transition from one assignment to the next without getting off track.

Sherialyn and I felt it was important for him to learn how to follow instructions and finish a task. So we decided to focus on helping him follow through, including a penalty if he got sidetracked from what he'd been told to do.

One evening I said, "Ricky, it's time for you to go upstairs and run your bath water right now." Ricky got right up, and I tell you, I was pretty proud. *Wow*, I thought. *He moved right on command.* Forty-five minutes later, I went upstairs to tell him good-night—and there was Ricky, fully clothed, sitting at the computer playing games.

I took immediate action. "Ricky, you didn't take your bath like I told you. No playing outside tomorrow." Now, we'd warned him what the penalty would be if he let himself get distracted from a task, and it was the worst penalty I could think of, because Ricky loved to play outside— riding his bicycle, practicing with his skateboard, just running around. So I wasn't too surprised when he stormed off to his room crying.

But I noticed that he was crying a lot longer than he normally did when given a penalty for rule violation. So I went into his room and said, "Why are you crying, Ricky? You knew what the penalty would be if you didn't follow through on what you were told to do."

"But, Dad!" Major wail. "I *did* do what you told me to do!"

"Now, wait a minute. I told you to go upstairs and take your bath. And instead you played computer games."

"No, you didn't, Dad!" Sobs and hiccups. "You told me to go upstairs and run my bath water. And that's what I did!"

I just looked at him. I had to admit, those were my very words: "Ricky, it's time for you to go upstairs and *run your bath water* right now." To my way of thinking, it was obvious that once you ran your bath water, you got in and took your bath. But to Ricky, it was sufficient to follow my instructions to the letter and then do something else.

I learned a valuable lesson that day: I had to get specific with my off- spring and clearly communicate what my expectations were!

IT'S A SHOW-AND-TELL

My experience with Ricky showed me that clear communication about rules or instructions sometimes includes *showing* what we mean, not just telling. After all, in coaching we don't just tell the players to do a triangle offense, we *show* them how to do it. We never took for granted that our players already knew how to rebound or double-team. A major part of coaching is demonstration, what we call a "walk through." Everything we taught the players followed this formula: Give clear instructions, demon- strate, walk through it, and practice. And it was important to do the walk- throughs at a pace that allowed them to clearly understand what we were asking them to do until they got the hang of it.

This coaching principle is no less important when you're teaching your kids to take care of various chores and tasks around the house. Why do we say, "Set the table" or "Clean out the garage" and then yell at them when they do it the wrong way? If we have expectations as to how something should be done, it's important to show them step by step how we want it done and then let them practice till they get the hang of it.

My wife and I had to go through this little drill especially when it came to asking our kids to clean up their rooms. They'd disappear into their bedrooms, then come out and say, "All done!" But when we inspected their rooms, they didn't even come close to our standard for a "clean room." When we found dirty laundry under the bed, Sherialyn and I realized we had to do a "walk through." So we actually cleaned their rooms with them, showing them step-by-step what we expected.

Once we did a walk-through, we saw tremendous improvement. Not perfection, mind you, but a definite improvement. And we've found that we have to do this literally with every task that we've given them to do. This isn't so strange when you think of discipline as teaching and training, not just rules and what to do if the rules get broken.

COMMUNICATING THE CONSEQUENCES

But face it, kids are kids and the rules will get broken. Part of teaching and training is helping our kids understand that poor choices and wrong behavior have consequences. Rather than throwing up our hands when our kids don't do what they're supposed to do, parents should see this as a teaching opportunity. After all, *un*disciplined kids often face *big* consequences in the game of life—especially if they end up with a sexually transmitted disease (STD), hooked on drugs, or facing a judge on a weapons charge.

When my coaching staff had a new team on our hands, we knew it was important not only to communicate the rules but also to communicate the consequences for breaking the rules. After all, this was college ball, a lot of the players were away from home for the first time, and we knew from experience (OK, OK, we were once college students, too!) the kinds of problems to expect from college students. It's typical for students to skip classes, to be late for classes, to occasionally chafe against authority. So we worked out what the consequences would be and told the team ahead of time that if they were late for team meetings, for instance, they'd have to run some wind sprints. They didn't like it when it was actually doled out, but they weren't surprised. The consequences for being late had been clearly communicated.

Why is this important in the family?

Clear communication of the consequences is beneficial for both the children and the parents. Too often parents react to misbehavior by dishing out the first punishment that comes to mind. But this is a problem on several levels. For one thing, the first penalty off the top of your head may not be the most effective consequence for the violation. For another, when we're not sure what penalty to give, too often we end up yelling and lecturing, which is the *least* effective discipline on earth. On the other hand, if we take action when we're upset, without thinking it through, we may do something we will later regret.

Another problem is inconsistency. If you scold Jeanette for interrupting while you're on the phone, but the next day you get upset and take away TV privileges from Jeremy *for the same offense*, your kids will think there's favoritism going on within the family. As far as you're concerned, Jeremy had just gotten on your *last* nerve! But the mind of a kid is going to think: *Mom loves Jeanette better than me.* This insecurity is especially a problem when one child in the family doesn't make many waves, while another child is rambunctious and is always getting called on the carpet.

Much better to tell your kids: "If you interrupt me while I'm on the phone, you'll have to take a fifteen-minute time-out. If you're late for supper, you'll do dishes by yourself. If you sass your mom, you're grounded to your room until you apologize." Everyone knows what the consequences are; everyone knows they'll be universally applied.

Of course, we can't anticipate *everything* our kids might do to get into trouble. Kids are pretty creative in that department. But a lot of things are typical of growing, immature kids that we as parents can anticipate and be prepared for: leaving toys out, teasing or hitting siblings, being late for meals, talking back, forgetting chores. If you communicate the consequences ahead of time for these (mis)behaviors, you and the kids both know that the penalty is fair. If Jeremy is late, he already knows what the consequence will be, and you don't even have to say much. (How often do we spoil the effectiveness of discipline by yelling and haranguing and lecturing, instead of allowing the penalty to speak for itself?)

Effective discipline not only communicates the expectations but also communicates the consequences.

EFFECTIVE CONSEQUENCES

Effective discipline is one of the most challenging areas of parenting. Too many parents are too busy and too tired to discipline effectively, much less talk about it ahead of time with their spouse. But failure to plan *effective discipline* results in kids playing one parent against the other ("If we ask Dad he'll say no, so let's ask Mom"). Or Dad will disagree with Mom's discipline in front of the kids. Pretty soon loyalty is strained, unity is strained, and order in the home is strained.

Another tendency is to use the same penalty for everything. Some parents ground their teenagers for everything from leaving wet towels on the bathroom floor to ignoring curfew. Another thinks "a spanking is the only thing a kid understands."

In reality, there are several different kinds of consequences that can be used effectively for different kinds of behavior. If we remember that *the overall purpose of discipline is really discipling, or training our children,* we will want to use consequences that are appropriate to the behavior or misbehavior and that will function as a teaching tool. These different types of consequences may include:

1. Time-Out

There's no question what time-out means during a game. The action has heated up on the floor and things are not going the way the coach wants them to go. Time out! Time out!

When a three-year-old is falling apart, won't cooperate, and nothing seems to be going right, a "time-out" for five or ten minutes may give enough time for the child to calm down and for Mommy to get a breather. Variations on the "time-out" (a child sits in a chair or is sent to another room to be alone) work for older children, too. It's a good way to give a child time to think and decide if he wants to cooperate. ("If you can't play without hitting, you will have to sit in this chair" or "As soon as you decide to say 'please' instead of yelling, you can come back to the table.") Many minor discipline problems can be handled with the judicious use of a time-out.

2. Reaping What Is Sown

Believe it or not, sometimes the most effective consequence is to *do nothing.* Kids learn responsibility when they experience the *natural consequences* of their actions and parents don't rush in to rescue them. Would you use "natural consequences" when your toddler is about to run into the street? Absolutely not! But if your eight-year-old dashes off to school without his lunch, doing nothing about it and letting him go hungry may help him to remember next time better than reminders, lectures, or punishments will.

Another time natural consequences might be most effective is when a teen has trouble getting up in the morning. This usually means missing the bus, and she ends up begging you for a ride. If you choose a natural consequence, *don't* nag her or wake her up (*do* give her an alarm clock, however); if she's late, *don't* take her to school (let her take a later bus); *don't* call in and excuse her for being late. A few unexcused tardies might mean she gets a detention, but let the school's discipline take its course.

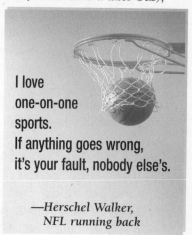

I love one-on-one sports. If anything goes wrong, it's your fault, nobody else's.

—*Herschel Walker, NFL running back*

You might deal with an *occasional* forgotten lunch or oversleeping with an act of grace by bringing the lunch or giving a ride. But ask yourself: are you always "nagging" or "rescuing"? (One teenager, tired of her mother's constant nagging, said, "Why should I remember to do anything? You do all my remembering for me.")

A good rule of thumb: If the consequences of a child's poor habits or decisions or actions primarily affect the child and will not permanently harm him or her, consider letting the natural consequences be the best teaching tool. (Doing nothing isn't as easy as it sounds! It'll probably mean biting your tongue, sitting on your hands, or going for a walk in order not to nag or rescue.)

3. Time to Fit the Crime

Many situations, however, don't have natural consequences built in. (Or the natural consequences affect others.) When Tiffany Teenager leaves wet towels, hair goo, and underwear all over the family bathroom, no parent is going to put up with the mess till the towels mildew. That's when we need to use *logical* consequences. Logical consequences are similar to natural consequences in that the "penalty" fits the "crime," except that the parent assigns a penalty that will help teach responsibility.

If Junior leaves his bicycle unlocked on the front lawn, you're probably not willing to allow the "natural" consequences to teach him a lesson by letting it get stolen. But you might put the bicycle away and tell him he can't ride it for a week.

One mom tackles the problem of her kids leaving their shoes and jackets lying all over the house by saying, "If I have to pick it up, it disappears for a week. Or if you really need it right away, you can buy it back for fifty cents."

Dr. Kevin Leman, a psychologist and family counselor, tells a great story[1] about the mother of a fussy eater who had tried everything—pleading, scolding, telling about the hungry kids in China, even giving the child something different than what the rest of the family was eating. Dad, on the other hand, thought all that cajoling was nonsense and simply banged his fist on the table and roared that the kid better eat or else! After consulting with Dr. Leman, the mother tried something new. One night Fussy Freddie took one look at the fried chicken strips (never a problem before) and pouted, "I hate it. I won't eat it." Instead of coaxing, Mom just said, "OK," took the plate of food, scraped it down the garbage disposal, and turned it on. Freddie stared in total disbelief. "You can get down from the table now," Mom said matter-of-factly. "See you at breakfast."

It was a short time from the first few garbage disposal incidences to Freddie's eating what was set before him. He learned that if he complained about the food, it simply disappeared, and there would be nothing till the next meal.

Isn't that a great story? (I can just hear scores of garbage disposals going off after parents read this chapter.) But the key to making logical consequences work is for parents to discuss a problem situation they're having with one of the kids and *decide together* what an effective consequence will be. Knowing you have a reasonable response to certain misbehaviors cuts out a lot of the unnecessary yelling and nagging and frustration. Be matter-of-fact, and let the consequence do the teaching.

4. Appropriate Spanking

There are times when a child is willfully disobedient or defiant and needs a wake-up call: "You've stepped way over the line, buddy, and that behavior won't be tolerated." In school, this kind of behavior usually results in a suspension—total removal; in professional sports, suspension and a heavy fine. But parents don't have this option. They can't

---

[1]Dr. Kevin Leman, *Making Children Mind Without Losing Yours* (Grand Rapids, Mich.: Fleming H. Revell, 1984). See pp. 81–83.

kick their kid out of the house.

My wife and I believe corporal punishment has a place in disciplining children, but we balance the rare occasions
we use spanking with a *lot* of hugging,
verbal affirmation, and expressions of
affection. Our kids know beyond a
shadow of a doubt that they are loved.
In that context, we believe an occasional spanking can be used to good effect.

Our kids know they will receive a
spanking if they are disrespectful to
adults, whether it's their parents, teach-

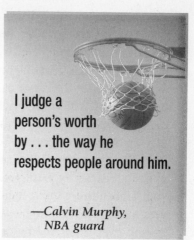

I judge a person's worth by . . . the way he respects people around him.

—*Calvin Murphy,*
NBA guard

ers, or neighbors. This not only includes talking back but also disrespectful actions, such as slamming a door. These things don't happen
very often in our house because our kids know in advance that they will
get a spanking for that type of behavior. Our kids also know that a spanking is forthcoming if they start a fight. They know that we do not condone fighting, and that this kind of behavior simply will not be tolerated.

Children shouldn't be spanked simply for being "childish"—running
in the house, forgetting to shut the refrigerator, getting mud on their
Sunday clothes. Other forms of discipline (training) help nudge our
children out of childishness toward more maturity. But we have found
that a spanking helps nip a defiant attitude and deliberate disobedience
in the bud—which means it doesn't have to be used very often. (I
would say that in a span of twelve years, our girls have only been
spanked three times.)

I'm not talking about slapping a kid around or giving him a beating.
No parent should take out his or her anger on a child. (The same
applies to screaming, name-calling, and belittling, which some parents
substitute for "corporal punishment," but these are actually more
destructive to a child's emotional well-being.)

As children grow older, other kinds of consequences are more
appropriate and effective. Unfortunately, a lot of children in our schools
today are out of control. Students talk back to teachers, ignore their
instructions, and disrupt the class. We are doing our children no favors
by tolerating that kind of behavior at home. An undisciplined child will
wreak havoc in his own life and in the lives of others. In the long run,
some "tough love" would be a lot more loving.

5. More Responsibilities

As children grow older, they should receive more privileges appropriate to their age. Being "fair" with our children doesn't mean we treat them exactly the "same." An older child should be able to stay up later, stay out longer, pick out their own clothes, have more say in family decisions.

But along with more privileges should also come more responsibilities. An older child may be asked to care for siblings, do their own laundry, cook a meal, shop for food, or wash the family car. (Though they should not be treated like convenient servants.)

This balance of *privileges and responsibilities* provides parents with a helpful training tool: If a child does not fulfill his or her responsibilities, certain privileges may be withdrawn. If our kids are negligent in cleaning up their rooms or doing their other household chores, we simply don't allow them to play their Nintendo games or watch a favorite television show or go outside to play, depending on what would be most effective with a particular child. (All three of our kids like to play outside more than anything, so having to stay inside is the penalty that hurts the most.)

We haven't hit the teen years big-time yet, but privileges and responsibilities can be an effective training tool during these transitional years. A teen driver who wants to drive the family car might be required to pay his or her own insurance, fill the car with gas, help keep it washed. Conversely, a teenager who takes the car without permission or gets the car home late could forfeit his driving privilege (a logical consequence). A teen who fails to complete her Saturday chores within the expected time could be denied the privilege of going to the mall or the movies. ("Please, Mom! I'll do them when I get back" almost always sets the stage for parental nagging and frustration later. If a parent holds firm that work comes before play, it's far more likely that the chores will get done *in time* next time.)

6. Reinforcement and Reward

Positive reinforcement and rewards can also be used to encourage appropriate behavior. Sometimes it can be as simple as saying, "Good job!" or "I really appreciate how you entertained the baby while I was on the phone." In other words, don't only notice when your kids do something wrong; give them credit when they do it right!

Rewards are a little trickier. An occasional reward can be a powerful incentive: "If you can pull that C up to a B, we'll go get that hoop you've been wanting." In these cases, the desired behavior must come first, *before* the reward. Don't fall into the trap of always "paying your kids to be good," and don't confuse rewards with bribery, such as, "OK, OK, I'll get that lollipop if you promise not to ask for anything else in the store." Soon the "bribe" is gone, and there's nothing to stop Little Princess from begging for something else.

ENFORCING THE RULES

As a coach, I knew that spelling out rules at the beginning of the year wouldn't accomplish *anything* if we didn't enforce them. If I told my players that they'd forfeit playing in the next game if they skipped classes, but I *didn't follow through*—how long do you think it would take before half the team would be skipping classes?

Seems like stating the obvious, doesn't it? Except in the home, *enforcing* the rules is often where discipline breaks down. Parents threaten dire consequences but don't mean it, or they're too tired to follow through. But my wife and I discovered a couple of other factors that make enforcing the rules a challenge.

(1) *Differences in the emotional makeup between men and women.* I don't want to over-generalize, but I think fathers tend to be more matter-of-fact about discipline, while mothers seem to have more empathy and are quick to pick up on the children's feelings. The good news is, this is a healthy balance. The Bible talks about not letting your children's tears keep you from disciplining them (Proverbs 19:18); but it also tells parents to not *provoke* their children to the point of anger and discouragement (Ephesians 6:4; Colossians 3:21). The strengths we bring as men and women to the family should complement each other, and this is one of the reasons God designed the family to ideally include a mom *and* a dad.

The bad news is, instead of letting our differences work together in balance, husbands and wives sometimes let their differences polarize them. They end up arguing over what the rules should be or whether the consequences are fair. If they can't agree, some parents end up not doing anything, or, out of frustration, one parent will impose a harsher penalty than is necessary. But this is where loyalty and unity on the "coaching staff" come into play. We need to keep in mind that our differences are actually a plus, and *for the good of the family team* we must make every effort not to let these differences polarize our relationship or undermine each other's discipline.

(2) *Most of us would rather avoid unpleasant situations.* As a coach, I never enjoyed making a player sit out a game. He was unhappy, I was unhappy, and sometimes his absence seriously handicapped our game. It is the same with the family. When my kids aren't happy, I am unhappy as well, and the whole family can be affected. Sometimes, rather than face the fallout I know is going to occur, it's tempting to back off— not so much to make my kids feel good, but because *I* don't want to feel bad and I don't want the family peace to be interrupted.

Both as a coach and as a parent, I've had to face the painful reality of enforcing consequences. It's not any fun! A lot of us probably heard our parents say, "This hurts me as much as it hurts you." *Yeah, right!* I didn't believe it then. But it's true. My kids have no idea that when I have to enforce a penalty, it definitely hurts me.

But something all parents should keep in mind is, if we don't discipline and train our children now, we are going to experience a lot more pain in the future. As difficult as it is to make my kids complete their chores, it's not as difficult as it would be in the future if they can't hold a job or support my grandchildren because they don't know how to stick with a task. Whenever I start to feel bad about disciplining one of my kids for breaking one of our family rules, it helps to think about the possibilities that await my child in the future if I *don't* correct this problem. If the police have to deal with a young person who's out of control; if an attitude problem or disrespect for authority makes it hard for him to hold down a job; if she develops harmful habits that keep her from being the best that she can be—that will bring a lot more pain in the future than the pain of being disciplined for a lesser offense now.

All the points we've touched on in this chapter will be effective, however, only if we parents are *consistent* in our discipline. Discipline can't depend on how we feel from one day to the next. It must be based on our own confidence that consistent, effective discipline is in the best interest of our children and grows out of our love for them.

INSTANT REPLAY

Bobby Knight, who has coached the Indiana Hoosiers for about three decades, says, "It has always been my thought that the most important single ingredient to success in athletics or in life is discipline. I have felt many times that this word is the most ill defined in all of our language. My definition of the word is as follows: (1) Do what has to be done, (2) when it has to be done, (3) as well as it can be done, and (4) do it that way all the time."[2] After coaching over a thousand games, he still expects his team to meet this standard because he knows that practice does not make perfect; practice makes permanent. Only perfect practice makes perfect.

Recently Coach Knight said,

> Without discipline there is no basis for trusting the parents' values or faith, and no respect for their viewpoints.
> —*John Perkins,*
> *racial reconciler*

> Basketball intrigues me as much as ever. Every season brings its new wrinkles—something different. Always something different. With me, it's not so much how well our players play, but how I can get them to play well. That part is getting harder and harder.

> If it were just me, I wouldn't have any problems. But it's not just me. It can be the parents. It can be the high school coaches. It can be the principals. Our kids of today are not getting the same lessons they used to. Very few are held accountable for what they do.

> Today, kids are always getting off the hook—someone is always finding a reason why they don't have to take responsibility for their actions, and that's wrong.[3]

As parents coaching our kids in the game of life, the stakes are high. Our kids need us—their first coach—to teach them, train them, disciple them, discipline them so that once they're on the playing floor of life, they can become all that they can be.

---

[2]Howard Ferguson, *The Edge* (Cleveland, Ohio: Getting the Edge Company, 1993), 3/12.

[3]Joe Falls, "Still Intense, Still Concerned, Bobby Knight Says Game Lacks Discipline and Commitment," *The Detroit News* Home Page, January 5, 1996.

FREE THROW

1. Discuss with your spouse—or with another parent if you're a single parent—how the concept of "discipling" your children (teaching, training, instruction) might change the way you approach the whole area of "discipline."

2. What is the most difficult aspect of discipline for you?
   • Understanding the difference between immature behavior that needs instruction, and disobedient behavior that needs correction?
   • Setting clear boundaries?
   • Effective consequences for rule violation?
   • Being consistent to enforce consequences?
   Why do you think this is the case? _____
   _____
   _____

3. Develop a plan of action for each of your children using the following chart.
   • Write each child's name in the column on the left.
   • In the second column, describe an area of discipline for each child that needs attention.
   • In the third column, decide on an appropriate consequence: "natural" consequence; "logical" consequence; spanking; withdrawing privileges or increasing responsibility (may overlap with logical consequences); or positive reinforcement or reward. (*Be specific.*)
   • In the fourth column, write the results. (Did you communicate clearly to your child? Did you follow through?)

Name of Child	Problem Area	Consequence	Results

9. KEEPING SCORE

Noncompetitive games may be politically correct, but in most games—and in life itself—scores count. Even if you are only competing against yourself, scores count. Every endeavor that is more than a pastime has a way of keeping score, a way to determine where you are in relation to where you want to be. Even the pay on your job over time is based on how you perform. Your headway on a trip is measured in miles. Even your health is evaluated in terms of numbers or scores. Scorekeeping matters.

Imagine watching a basketball game or a football game or any sport in which there was no scorekeeping. Suppose the teams just played until dark, and that was it. Do you think the players would be as motivated to play? Do you think you would be as interested in watching? Can you imagine a sellout crowd packing the United Center to watch the Bulls in 1998 if there would have been no scorekeeping, if they were not contending for their sixth NBA championship? Why would Michael Jordan even bother to "fly" so high?

Keeping score matters!

And yet many tend to show little or no interest in their kids' "scores" until they've "lost" in some tragic way. Just as in sports, your kids' lives tend to lose relevancy if you show no interest in the scores. Even though they may complain that you keep too close tabs on them, don't be fooled. If you didn't pay attention to how they were doing, in effect, you would be telling them that you didn't care about them.

THE VALUE OF KEEPING SCORE

We keep score so that we are not caught by surprise at the outcome, and we keep score to instill motivation for greater achievement.

In a sporting contest, it is easy to keep score because the score is illuminated right in front of you on a big scoreboard, one of the largest pieces of equipment at the game. In fact, usually there are several scoreboards throughout the arena so that everyone can see the score at a glance.

As far as the fans are concerned, constant access to the score maintains interest in the contest.

As far as the coaches and players are concerned, the score often determines the next play, sometimes leading to some very unusual strategies.

Imagine a close basketball game with fifty-three seconds remaining in the fourth quarter and only two points separating the teams. When the leaders take possession, they may not even try to score. Instead, they may pass the ball around in the backcourt to run time off the clock.

Likewise, the team that's down may intentionally foul the leaders, hoping they will miss their free throws, giving the followers a chance to tie up the game on their next possession. Or, who knows, there might be a steal and a chance to win.

These would be unthinkable strategies at any other time in the game, but given the score and the remaining time, they are smart moves.

As a coach, I was constantly looking at the scoreboard. I cannot recall a time during a game in which I did not know the score. Even the players need to know the score every minute of the game, and that includes more than the points. It includes everything that might affect the outcome of the game.

For instance, at the end of the 1993 NCAA championship game, Michigan's star player, Chris Webber, rebounded a North Carolina missed foul shot and dribbled toward his team's bench and Coach Steve Fisher. There, Webber stopped and signaled for a time-out. It seemed a smart move. With eleven seconds remaining, the Wolverines could reset and run a play that might throw the 73–71 contest into overtime or even win the game with a three-pointer. The only problem was, Michigan was out of time-outs!

"Technical foul!"

The Tar Heels sunk their foul shots and took possession. In desperation, Michigan fouled them again, but North Carolina hit those shots as well, icing the score 77–71 to take home the championship.

Not knowing the "score" can cost you dearly. After the game, Coach Steve Fisher said, "Apparently we didn't get specific enough [that there were no more time-outs]. I'm the guy who should have been sure everyone knew."[1]

> **It's what you learn after you know it all that counts.**
>
> —*John Wooden, college basketball coach*

Even though knowing the score in sports seems basic, I was often amazed when I went into various homes on recruiting visits to discover how many parents didn't know the "score" concerning their own kids. They were completely surprised when we pointed out that their son had been having academic difficulties or behavioral problems in high school. You can't plan your next play or take corrective measures if you don't know the score.

But paying attention to the score serves another purpose. Our attention to the score motivates our "players." They are aware whether or not you check the score. If you do, they know their participation matters to you, and your interest motivates them to do their best.

Suppose your daughter comes home from school with an assignment that she has completed and you do not show any interest in it. That kind of response almost guarantees the child's interest in future assignments will be diminished. If her work is not important to you, it will not be important to your child.

HOW DO YOU KEEP SCORE?

In sports there is a scoreboard that is easy for all to see, and there are statistics that record the details of each player's performance. In life, it is not always so easy to see how a child is doing. Obviously there is the periodic report card from school, and if you are the least bit attentive,

---

[1]Skip Myslenski, "Carolina Enjoys 'T' Party: One Time-out Too Many Fatal for Michigan," *Chicago Tribune*, Sports, April 6, 1993, 1.

you know whether other adults—teachers, neighbors, even the police—have been complaining about your child's behavior. But when these reports come to your attention, it is often too late.

What are the early warning signs for how well a child is doing? When is "Kids will be kids!" a fool's platitude, and when is it the response of a wise parent?

Academic progress. It always alarms me to find out how many parents do not participate in parent/teacher conferences. They assume that their child's report card is all they need to see the academic score. But that's like thinking you can coach a game by looking at the scoreboard only at the end of each quarter!

Depending on the need, there are many ways to monitor how your kids are doing in school. Pay attention to their assignments, their homework, and papers they bring home. Go over these things daily, affirming your child's good efforts, rejoicing when efforts result in good grades, sharing in disappointments when they don't (this is different than scolding), and hold your child accountable for doing his or her homework. If they are vague about assignments or seem confused about them, try recording what they are in a notebook for a time to keep track of what is done and what isn't.

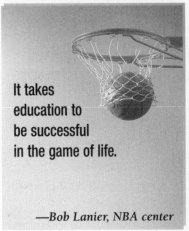

It takes education to be successful in the game of life.

—*Bob Lanier, NBA center*

When a friend of mine discovered at a parent/teacher conference that his son wasn't turning in his homework (even though he usually did it), the father arranged with the teacher to initial a card each day to indicate that his son had followed through. No initial on the card meant no TV that night.

Most teachers are even willing to receive phone calls from concerned parents if that will help a kid keep up with schoolwork.

Why such concern for academics?

Certainly school isn't everything, but for most of the year school is the "work" expected of kids. Falling behind at school can be indicative of falling behind in life. You will want to pay regular attention to that score, and not just when report cards come out. Your interest in their work is one of the most important expressions of your interest in your children. And it tells them that you consider school to be very important.

Body language. My mother used to say, "Don't look at me with that tone of voice," and I knew exactly what she meant. You've experienced it—someone tells you one thing while his or her body language says something different. Facial expressions, tone of voice, and how a person stands or sits give us accurate information about what's happening inside that person—even more, sometimes, than their words do. Why is this so? One reason is because these expressions do not require the same accountability as words do. The other reason is that body language and voice inflection are often unconscious. We express ourselves in this way without thinking.

If you really don't know the score—and I'm convinced that all too often parents have a pretty good idea; they just don't know what to do

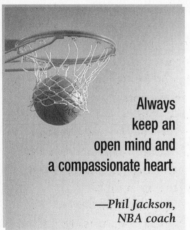

Always keep an open mind and a compassionate heart.

—Phil Jackson, NBA coach

about it or they don't have the energy to do anything about it—then commit yourself to gently discovering the truth.

Often when I come home from work, I can tell—based on the facial expressions of my kids—that something has not gone right at school or at home. A little sleuthing—if I'm genuine in wanting to know—usually reveals the cause. Then I get the opportunity to help them navigate through those difficult situations. It is true that I occasionally ignore what I see, but that should be a conscious decision—possibly a refusal to be manipulated by a pout—not laziness or lack of concern on my part.

On the other hand, if my kids greet me with smiles and joy, then I can usually assume that they are "up" in the score of life. When we look at the scoreboard during a contest and see we are up five or six points, that makes us feel good. But when we are down, we know that something needs attention.

The way a kid holds his or her head is a real clue as to how they feel inside. I am not saying you need to make a big deal of it every time you see your child with her head down, but be alert so that discouragement doesn't set in. Let your kids know you care how they feel.

One of the things that coaches often say to their players is, "Keep your head up." For some reason, the head-up posture gives your opponents the impression that you are confident about what you are getting ready to do. If your head is down, you telegraph that you feel defeated even before the contest has begun. If a kid is shuffling along with his head down, that should tell you something about how he feels. Try to find out the cause before merely saying, "Chin up, shoulders back, quit shuffling!"

Tone of voice often conveys more than actual words. As a coach, if I gave a kid a set of instructions and then asked him if he understood, I paid particular attention to *how* he said, "Yes, Coach, I understand." He might have understood, but his tone of voice was the key to how enthusiastically he was going to follow though. If we are going to be good scorekeepers in coaching our kids in the game of life, we must be acutely tuned to all the ways they are telling us what's going on in their lives.

Pay especially close attention to all these signals when your kids are young and you can read them with a fair amount of accuracy. In this way you will communicate to your kids that they matter to you. You may even encourage more verbal "score reports" from them and in this way avoid their learning to hide what's going on inside. Too often parents of teenagers say their kids are completely unreadable, but kids don't get that way overnight. It usually results from years of experiencing one of two reactions from their parents: Either parents did not pay attention to the signals when the kids were young, so the kids gave up transmitting them, or, at the other extreme, the parents came down so harshly that the kids learned to mask their feelings entirely.

Let me point out that these ways of reading your kids' "score" are ways we coaches used to keep score on our team members. In other words, we learned a lot about whether our guys were prepared to play in a game based on these same indicators.

Note the company they keep. As I mentioned before, rarely have I seen a kid get into trouble entirely on his own. Usually it requires a group of kids to generate the courage (or the foolishness, as the case may be) to try something he knows is wrong. In eighteen years of coaching, almost every time a kid on my team got into trouble, it was because he got mixed up with kids who were not on the team. They drew him into activities that were not team-related or healthy for him. This is not to excuse the team member as though he were helpless to say no. But it does identify where and when that "no" should be exercised. In most cases it is *before* seriously associating with the wrong company. I can't stress it enough: Pay attention to who your kids are associating with.

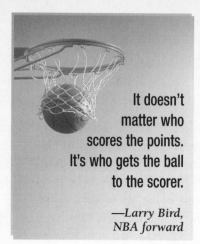

It doesn't matter who scores the points. It's who gets the ball to the scorer.

—Larry Bird, NBA forward

And to get to know them, you need access to them. The best way we've discovered for doing that is, as I mentioned earlier, to establish our home as the place where kids in the neighborhood can and want to play. We are always open to kids playing with our kids in our home. Of course, this can sometimes be a challenge. We may not like the noise or the mess that extra kids bring into our home, but I think the trade-off is worth it. It gives us a good sense of who our kids are hanging out with, and, even if some kids whom we might consider "marginal" in terms of behavior are in our home, our values dominate. And we don't apologize for that! If we can help it, we are not going to allow things to happen in our home that we consider inappropriate.

Having first gotten acquainted with our kids' friends in our home, my wife and I have a sense of who they are before we allow our kids to go into their homes to play or to spend the night. We don't expect everyone to believe the same way we do, but the bottom line is that our kids are our responsibility, and the things that are likely to influence them are our also responsibility. If our kids are going to spend any extended time in someone else's home, we make it our business to meet the parents and discover whether there will be appropriate supervision in that home.

Pay attention to the influence of other advisors. Know who your kids consider role models and advisors. Do they have a value system you can affirm? Not all confusion among youth comes from peers or the media. Sometimes other adults, other informal advisors, even people your kids look up to who may be only a few years older—all these can have a tremendous impact on your kids. You need to know the score.

When coaching basketball, I noticed that as players got older—usually when they became seniors—they tended to look elsewhere for guidance. Sometimes they were thinking about a job or grad school or the NBA or marriage. Of course, their looking to others for guidance at these points was natural and sometimes in their best interest, but I needed to know the "score" if it was going to affect their participation on the team.

Do they have good friends? We talked earlier about keeping score concerning how peers influence your kids, but it is just as important to note whether your kids have some *good* friends. We don't want them to feel isolated, either.

At one time our daughter Sabrina seemed to be more comfortable by herself. Now, there's nothing wrong with that if it represents a child's temperament rather than a lack of confidence or feelings of rejection. So we kept a watch on it, occasionally encouraging her to make new friends or find someone to spend time with. Then we began to see a change in her. She accepted our encouragement and soon had friends over, as well as asking to spend the night at their homes. So that aloneness has turned around, but we were aware of it, watching to see if it would change.

DON'T MICROMANAGE

Keeping a constant eye on the scoreboard doesn't mean you have to micromanage everything your children do. Every time a coach looks up at the scoreboard, he does not stop the game to make changes. Out of an entire forty-minute college basketball game, the coach gets only about five minutes during time-outs, plus half time, to do any correcting, encouraging, or strategizing with the team. If we could see life in that same context, we would understand that there are only a few strategic opportunities to guide our kids along the course that we want for them. So choose your battles wisely. Make them count, especially as your children get older. If we try to turn our "five time-outs" into fifteen, our kids may grow tired of hearing our voice and become bored with the game. Nevertheless, a good coach always knows the score, and that reassures the players because *they* know that *he* knows the score.

Have you ever watched children playing in a yard while their parents stood and watched? Half the time the children are glancing to see if Mom and Dad are still there. Now, they are not expecting correction or affirmation all the time, but it matters to them that someone is watching. Many times it

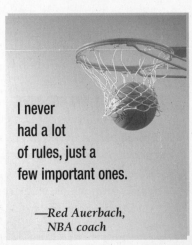

I never had a lot of rules, just a few important ones.

—*Red Auerbach,*
NBA coach

makes them bold enough to try something new because they trust that Mom or Dad will stop them if it is something out of bounds or dangerous. This approach should continue throughout their growing up years, encouraging them as coaches; not looking to curtail their fun, but to be there for support or help when needed.

A good coach watches the scoreboard so that at some future time he can point out *why* the score is what it is—whether favorable or not so favorable. If as a coach to your children you react to everything that happens on "the court," in time, you may create tremendous friction between yourself and your kids.

During the 1991–92 season when the Chicago Bulls' started out 36–3, Jerry Reinsdorf wanted to know whether Coach Phil Jackson was driving the team toward the Lakers' record of 69–3. Jackson told him no, it was out of his hands. Later he wrote, "When everything is running smoothly, I . . . try to leave few traces. . . . This is what I'd been striving for ever since I started coaching: to become an 'invisible' leader."[2]

Especially as our kids get older, our coaching needs to become more invisible. We don't want them to be so tired of hearing our voice that they tune us out. At that age, it's better to be there, always know the score, but not make an issue of every point during the game.

I have also found it valuable to trust my spouse with timing in bringing any serious correction. Like a wise assistant coach, my wife is often more in touch with something that is happening with our kids than I am. She may have a better perspective on what is needed or she may be watching for a more strategic time to step in.

This is particularly important if you are going to adopt the method of not making an issue of every problem. You and your "coaching staff" need to communicate and agree on such changes so that one of you isn't accused of neglect or of not caring.

PLAYING WHEN YOU ARE DOWN

Coaches know that at some time in every contest their team is likely to be behind. Only rarely will you lead from buzzer to buzzer. So it is important to keep your attitude positive, even when your team's scoring has slowed down. Don't get discouraged; see it as part of the game, a phase from which your team *can* rebound.

What happens far too often is that we see certain things happening

---

[2]Phil Jackson, *Sacred Hoops* (New York: Hyperion, 1995), 160.

in the lives of our kids that make us fear we've "lost the game." A kid might make a poor grade in math, and we think the doors to business, science, and medicine have all slammed shut simultaneously. This is too drastic a conclusion for merely noticing that your kid is behind in the game. Just like coaches, parents need to understand that there are going to be periods in a child's life when he is behind, but he *can* come back.

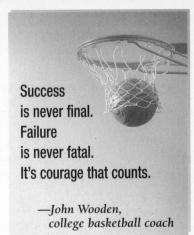

Success is never final. Failure is never fatal. It's courage that counts.

—*John Wooden,*
college basketball coach

There's an old adage that applies equally well to coaching and to parenting: "Catch 'em being good!" It works for two reasons. (1) When children are young, much of their behavior—whether good or bad—is designed to engage their parents' attention. Of course, they would prefer to receive their parents' approval, but if they can't get that, they will settle for disapproval, just so long at they get their attention. Catching children at being good helps reinforce positive behavior, while you can sometimes discourage bad behavior by ignoring it. (2) As they get older, catching children at being good is one of the most effective ways of letting them know that you are still on their side. Even when they are down, you can always find something to affirm. Kids have a tremendous fear of failure, and the older they get, the more they are aware when "the score" looks bad. They know when they are down, and one of the things they need most at that moment is your confidence that they can rebound. Encouraging them in an area of competence tells them that you are on their side; you haven't abandoned them; they can make it!

Being behind isn't "wrong." You just need to come up with a strategy to turn the game around. If you act as though the whole game is already lost, one of two things is likely to happen. First, your kids will develop a tremendous fear of failure because they know the backlash they will get from you. That fear can cause them to avoid trying, so that their true capacity or weaknesses aren't exposed.

Second, *you* may lose your motivation to coach if falling behind becomes too big a deal for you. It is important that you as a parent continue to see a positive potential even in the midst of negative figures. In other words, when you look at the scoreboard, and your "team" is down, you need to remember that there is still a game to be played. The

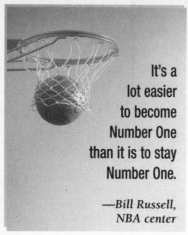

It's a lot easier to become Number One than it is to stay Number One.

—Bill Russell, NBA center

scoreboard is still on. The game is not over. Any team can keep playing when they are ahead, but they need a real coach when they fall behind. So don't panic. Coach them to a moral victory if not a numeric one.

What's still possible even when a total victory is out of reach? Two things: toughness and momentum. If you play on through, then you've proved that defeat cannot defeat your team! Also, if you can generate a rally, even in the last few minutes, it will carry into the next game and give you an advantage there.

The score must not create a defeatist attitude in us. Never! If it does, it will swamp our kids.

As coaches, the score is only meant to give us information for how we can adjust and make the score whatever we would like it to be before the game is over.

INSTANT REPLAY

The scoreboard, in and of itself, doesn't tell the whole story about whether your team is winning. There is another element: time. Being down five points early in the game is a lot different than being down five points late in the game. It's very hard, but most great coaches continue to coach with the same passion regardless of what the score is until the game is over. Remember this with your kids: The game is never over until it is over.

Midway through his 1974 season, major league baseball pitcher Tommy John's arm totally gave out on him. He underwent a revolutionary elbow surgery procedure in which he had a tendon transplanted from his right forearm to his left elbow to fix a tear. His doctor said that he would never pitch again. He was down, and it looked like he was out.

Yet Tommy John said, "You're a great doctor, and I believe in you. But you're wrong. I won't quit. I will come back!"

He missed the remainder of that season and all of 1975, but he returned and won twenty games three times in the next five years. The procedure he underwent is now relatively common among profession-al pitchers and known as "Tommy John surgery."

Whether the score is good or bad, at some strategic points along the way in life, you need to remind your kids that there is a lot more of life still to come—a lot more time on the clock. No matter how things are going right now—good or bad—they shouldn't rest on their laurels or quit trying. As long as there is life flowing inside a person, there is a chance to turn things around.

FREE THROW

The following list of behaviors could be warning signs in terms of reading the "score," especially with teenagers. They are not equally important. Most teens, for instance, complain of insufficient freedom. But other signs are more critical, and certainly if your teen "scores" on several of them, it might be good to seek assistance. Put a check by all that apply.

____ Acts excessively selfish
____ Behaves seductively
____ Carries a weapon
____ Ceases to bring friends home
____ Changes appearance dramatically
____ Complains about insufficient freedom
____ Conceals whereabouts/activities
____ Criticizes "straight" kids
____ Defends people who use drugs
____ Displays or draws gang symbols
____ Drops out of sports or other activities
____ Engages in binge drinking

List continued next page

____ Experiences extreme weight loss or gain
____ Exhibits defensiveness about friends
____ Exhibits a negative personality change
____ Explodes in violent behavior or speech
____ Expresses hostility toward police
____ Gets a tattoo of a gang symbol
____ Has friends you've never heard of
____ Is expelled from school
____ Is fired from after-school job
____ Is involved in group fights
____ Is sexually active
____ Lies and searches for loopholes
____ Misses school or is tardy
____ Mutilates self
____ Often seems depressed
____ Possesses drug paraphernalia
____ Pulls away from the family emotionally
____ Receives lower-than-usual grades
____ Receives secretive phone calls
____ Refuses to use a seat belt
____ Resists family values
____ Runs away from home
____ Smokes
____ Stays out all night
____ Steals things
____ Talks about dropping out of school
____ Talks about suicide
____ Uses a street name
____ Uses alcohol frequently
____ Uses hand signs with friends
____ Valuables disappear from home
____ Vandalizes things
____ Violates curfew but with "good" excuses
____ Wears clothing of only certain colors

2. Are you micromanaging your children's lives? Ask your spouse or a close friend to monitor how you supervise your kids for one hour (or longer if you can arrange it). Have the other person note both how many directives you issue as well as what they are. Then sit down

together and go over those notes.

- How many directives were essential for your child's safety, well-being, or the accomplishment of a task?
- How many were unnecessary, meaning your child probably would have done OK without your intervention?
- If you tend toward micromanaging or nagging, consider how you might reduce your input. Are you trying to protect your children from natural consequences that could teach them better?

3. For each child, identify one area in which his or her "score" is down. Then identify one area where you can encourage your child by "catching 'em being good." When you communicate your affirmation, be sure to say, "That was a good job you did on . . ." or "I appreciate how you . . ." rather than, "You're such a good girl. You make Mom so happy." The first encourages the child by identifying a behavior that can be duplicated and multiplied. The latter loads the child with a burden that he or she may feel unable to live up to, especially if they are keenly feeling bad about being down in some other area.

10. REBOUNDING MAKES MVPS

I know the men's basketball team at Northwestern already thought I was a little bit crazy. But I just hauled that ladder out onto the practice floor, snapped it open next to the hoop, and sent my assistant coach, Shawn Parrish, scrambling to the top. Then I handed up a big plastic "lid" that Shawn snapped down on the rim of the hoop, covering the net.

"All right, gentlemen," I said as Shawn hustled back down the ladder. "Rebound practice."

We called that lid "the bubble," and it served a useful purpose: it sent every ball shot toward the hoop bouncing right back out, again and again. The players never had the satisfaction of seeing the ball drop through the net. Rather, they had to quickly get in position to take possession and shoot again.

"Rebound! Rebound! Rebound!" I prodded loudly from the sidelines.

Rebounding is an integral part of the whole game of basketball—not just a play the coach pulls out in case of emergency. Simply put, *rebounding means to retrieve a missed opportunity*. My staff and I built rebounding skills into all our practice drills. It didn't matter if it was a defensive drill or an offensive drill. We wanted each player to be prepared for the missed shot, whether by their own team member or by their opponent, and know how to turn it into an opportunity to score.

I'm serious. Games are won or lost right here.

From a coaching point of view, I wanted to develop in my team the *capacity* to rebound. It's a positioning issue—how to put yourself in position to rebound. It's also an attitude issue—how do you respond to missing that lay-up or when a teammate risks a three-point shot and misses? Do you let a missed shot throw you off your game? Or do you see how to turn that missed shot into another offensive opportunity?

Frankly, rebounding takes both hustle and heart, qualities that may very well earn a player the title Most Valuable Player (MVP).

Hustle and heart. What are we parents doing to prepare our kids to rebound from a supposed failure? How do they respond when "the opposition" blocks their best shot? Even when the competition has the upper hand, are your kids prepared to turn a defensive rebound into an offensive score, or are they just going to stand there and grin because the other guy missed?

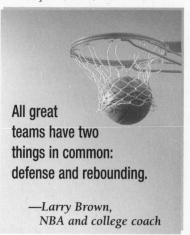

All great teams have two things in common: defense and rebounding.

—*Larry Brown,*
NBA and college coach

The game of life might be won or lost right here. It's all about your family team's capacity to rebound, to retrieve those lost opportunities.

REALISTIC EXPECTATIONS: SHOTS WILL BE MISSED

In most basketball games, roughly 50 percent of all shots will be missed. Surprised? You shouldn't be. Coaches and players know that's just reality. It doesn't matter how hard you work or how much you know, some shots just aren't going to drop. That's why a good team is prepared to rebound—to take some of those misses and turn them into scores.

Of course all players—and coaches—want that ball to go into the hoop the first time. That's why on basketball courts, playground slabs, and garage driveways all over the country, basketball players and wannabes practice lay-ups, jump shots, slam dunks, and three-pointers. But any good coach will help his players deal with reality: Do your best to make the shot, but prepare to follow up if you miss.

The game of life is no different. You have hopes and expectations for your children, but things will not always go as planned. Is the game over? Or do we help our children rebound and make the most of the next opportunity?

Some people might have trouble *preparing* their kids for when things go wrong. But take a clue from the typical toddler. I watched in fascination when my first little girl, Sabrina, was just learning to walk. She took a big risk and let go of the sofa. She fell down. She picked herself up. She took two steps and fell down again. She picked herself up. Up, down. Up, down. Pretty soon she was walking. Were all those plops onto her bottom failures? Of course not. She rebounded.

It's not so much expecting things to go wrong as learning how to respond in a constructive way when they do.

We do our kids a big favor when we encourage them to try, to make their best effort, and if they don't "score" the first time around, to figure out how they can turn the "miss" into another opportunity.

Both of our daughters play the piano quite well. Our oldest, Sabrina, had gotten a "Superior" rating a couple of years in a row at a city-wide music festival, and each time had been invited back to participate in a public recital. Then one year both Sabrina and Kelley got a "Superior" rating—but only Kelley was invited to participate in the recital. Sabrina felt very discouraged. It was all over. She was ready to quit piano lessons. To her, the Superior rating didn't count; being invited back to give a recital was what counted. It took some serious encouragement on our part before she understood that only so many musicians could participate in the recital. She'd had several opportunities; now it was time for others to have a turn. She was doing very well in piano and shouldn't give up. Finally she was able to deal with her disappointment and move on.

But sincere efforts that don't quite make it aren't the only kinds of "missed shots" kids need to be prepared to deal with. In this chapter, I'd like to also deal with the mistakes kids make—the bad decisions, poor judgments, wrong choices. These might include a wide range of "misses":

- watching TV instead of doing homework
- going to a party without parents' permission
- disrespecting a teacher
- telling a lie
- shoplifting (from candy to clothes)
- experimenting with drugs

- driving while drinking
- a teen pregnancy

Of course, we need to teach our kids to make good decisions and right choices, and to give them plenty of practice. We can hold a high standard and even expect them to reach it, but since none of us are perfect parents—and I haven't yet met the perfect kid—we also need to teach them what to do when they make a mistake, when they miss the mark. If we don't have realistic expectations, we won't practice our rebounding skills as a family team and we'll miss the opportunity to turn that miss into a score.

GETTING IN POSITION TO REBOUND

When I'm working with a team on rebounding, the first thing I tell my players is that, even before a shot goes up, they must act quickly and *get in position to rebound*. They can do this best with a tactic known as *boxing out* the opposition. It is exactly what it sounds like: They create a human "box" with their bodies under the basket that prevents their opponents from getting close enough to grab a rebound.

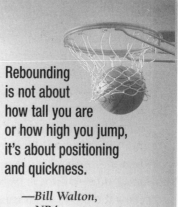

Rebounding is not about how tall you are or how high you jump, it's about positioning and quickness.

—*Bill Walton,*
NBA center

First, they need to move to the basket-side of their opponents and turn so that they are facing the goal. Then they squat down with their arms out from their sides, making themselves as wide as possible to prevent an opponent from getting around them. When two or three players do this effectively, they are in the best position to control the board. Effective execution depends on three things, and they each have their real-life counterparts:

1. *Knowing where your opponent is.* It is obvious in basketball that you have to know where your opponents are before you can box them out. But in life it is the same. You need to know what your personal obstacles are or you'll never get ahead of them.

2. *Everyone on the team doing his or her job.* In life as in basketball, rebounding is a team effort. There will be times when you as a parent will need to help create the space for your kid to grab the rebound. There will be times when you need to shoot her an "outlet pass" so she

can have a second chance at making her goal.

3. *Applying what you've learned before.* In other words, the team spirit, scouting the enemy's weaknesses, knowing the rules of the game, practicing the skills and drills, the discipline, knowing the game plan, knowing the score—all contribute to getting that second chance known as a rebound.

Everything you build into your family as the family coach—the love, unity, discipline, knowing the rules, setting goals, scouting what the challenges are going to be—all increase the likelihood that your kid, or the family as a whole, can get in position to rebound when mistakes are made. It's important that your family understands that *everyone* in the family plays a role in helping a family member rebound. And then you've got to put in that extra effort to make it happen. You can't let fatigue glue you to the floor.

Suppose you get home from grocery shopping and discover that your six-year-old is eating candy you didn't buy. It might be tempting to just scold him, send him to his room, and let it go at that. After all, it's only worth a dollar, and you're tired. But you'd be missing an opportunity to turn this "miss" into a second chance.

It would be better to take away any uneaten candy, put your little shoplifter back in the car, drive to the grocery store, hunt up the manager, and tell your kid to apologize. Pay for the candy and deduct it from the child's allowance. Maybe deduct double. Then call the whole family together and go over the rules and consequences for stealing. Warn the other kids not to tease the culprit or talk about it outside the family. If the culprit is truly sorry, be sure to express your own forgiveness—and God's forgiveness, too.

You've just boxed out the opposition and put your kid in position to rebound, because there will come another time in that grocery store, or when he's older and is passing that coveted pair of Nikes, or . . . who knows what?

ANALYZING MISSES

As outrageous as Dennis Rodman's behavior is, you gotta admit he's a rebound master. When he played for the Chicago Bulls, Rodman spent hours studying the videotapes of opposing teams and analyzing which players shot the ball from where, and at what angle the ball bounced if it didn't go in. He knew full well that a shot from the free-throw line was going to come off the rim at a different angle than a lay-up from the baseline. And when that ball came off the rim, Rodman was there.

As the family coach, you can help your kids analyze missed shots as well. The mistakes of others can be a teaching tool—you don't have to wait until your own kid messes up:

"Hey, sport, heard a couple of the guys got kicked off the team for testing positive for drugs. Wasn't one of them your friend Matt?"

"Yeah. But I think the school overreacted. Matt's a senior, Dad! Probably going to lose his athletic scholarship."

There is no glory in rebounding . . . just victory.

—*George Raveling, college basketball coach*

"He had a lot to lose. Why do you think he risked it?"

"Aw, it was that party last weekend at Charlie Smith's house. Heard someone showed up with a lot of beer and weed, and . . . guess it kinda got out of hand."

"The Smiths allowed drinking and marijuana at their house?" Trying to keep the shock and outrage out of your voice.

"Duh, Dad! Of course not!" Rolled eyes at the hopeless ignorance of the adult species. "Charlie's parents were out of town."

"So . . . why didn't Matt just refuse?"

Look of scorn. "Just say no? It's not that easy, Dad, when everyone else is doing it."

"So . . . how could Matt have avoided what happened?"

Shrug. "Guess he could've left when the booze and blunts showed up."

"Still, that was pretty risky, attending an unsupervised party as a minor. What other choices did Matt have?"

"Well . . . not go to the party, I guess."

"Was that the only alternative?"

"Have the party at somebody else's house whose parents were home?"

"Or. . . ?"

"OK, Dad, I know what you're driving at. I invited Matt to shoot some pool over here and he turned me down. So he had some choices."

"Right. There are always choices. And choices have consequences."

Talking through situations they know about from school, or even
stories in the newspaper, can help your kids discover where the "decision points" are that make the difference between a "missed shot" and
putting themselves in position to score. But it's especially important to
do this if your own kid is the one who missed the shot. What could
they have done differently? What can they do differently next time?

I'll never forget the day Sherialyn told me about picking up Ricky Jr.
from preschool only to learn that he had hit his teacher.

"He *what*?" I asked, astounded.

"Well, according to her," Sherialyn said, "he actually hit her in the
face."

I found this hard to believe. Ricky had his share of preschool squab-
bles with other kids, and the classroom did have a lot of feisty little boys
in it, but to my knowledge, he had never hit an adult. What we learned,
however, is that Ricky and a classmate had gotten into a fight, and the
other boy hit Ricky first. But before Ricky could hit him back, the
teacher intervened—so Ricky's punch hit the teacher! (All wound up
and no place to go.)

It was a good teaching moment. We spent some time helping Ricky
understand why it happened ("Did you mean to hit the teacher?" "No,
I wanted to hit [the kid], but she stopped me, so I hit her!"). Then we
taught him some constructive ways to handle his emotions ("Use words
to say how you feel instead of hitting").

Just by asking these questions, you show faith that your kid *is* capable of using good judgment and making a good decision next time.

REBOUNDING STRATEGIES

Analyzing missed shots is one "rebounding strategy." But there are
others: *following the shot* (the shooter who missed the shot follows the
ball and grabs it on the rebound); *boxing out* (as described earlier: moving from the defensive position—facing the opponent, and pivoting
into a position where the player can keep his eye on the ball—back to
opponent); *calling for a time-out* (in critical situations, like the end of a
game).

As a parent, I can help my kids learn how to "follow the shot" by giving them lots of opportunities to try and fail and try again. Let your kids

stretch a little beyond their reach. We need to communicate the attitude that it's OK to fail. I'm talking primarily about efforts to try new things at which they might not succeed initially—a new sport, new friends, a new class, a new skill—not poor choices that lead to wrong actions.

> I've scored 20,000 points, but the thing I'm most proud of is my rebounding record.
>
> —*Charles Barkley, NBA forward*

And if they fail at something new, there is your opportunity to teach them how to rebound, to learn from their mistakes and try again. Sometimes kids miss chances to rebound because their eyes are on all the obstacles. This is where we've got to help them pivot in the middle of the situation, put the obstacles to their back, and focus on the goal. (This doesn't mean they don't have to deal with the obstacles, but they shouldn't become preoccupied or overwhelmed by them.)

Suppose you heard those dreaded words, "Daddy, I . . . I'm pregnant." And she's only fifteen! I know that in that moment most parents would probably *feel* like the game's over. "All my hopes and dreams for my child . . . lost." But even in the worst setbacks you can think of, the game is *not over*. It's going to be tough. It's going to take the whole family team to rebound from this one. But the best coaching you could give your child in that situation is to help her refocus on the goal—her goals, the family goals. A teen pregnancy is a big mistake, surely. But it's not a fatal mistake. Even if it costs the game at hand, it's not the end of the season.

In a situation like this, a family time-out to regroup, to discuss what went wrong, to get spiritual counsel, to plan the best strategy is entirely appropriate. When you figure out what went wrong ("analyzing the missed shot"), it might mean retraining, changing positions, even a whole new game plan. But the opportunity to rebound is still there.

DEFENSIVE REBOUNDS—WHEN OTHERS MISS THE SHOT

Sometimes it's our team that misses the shot; other times it's "the other guy." If our opponent takes a bad shot, are we going to stand there reveling in his mistake, or are we going to grab the rebound and head for our goal? One of the most important things we can teach our children is that *they* are not responsible for the actions and mistakes of other people, but they *are* responsible for how they respond to those actions.

Here our example as parents is key. In fact, they may learn more by observing how we respond than by what we say. In other words, spouting off, "He made me *so* mad" as an excuse for why you rammed the car of a discourteous driver doesn't cut it. The other driver didn't *make* you be mad. He was discourteous, but you got mad about it *all by yourself.*

Sometimes the mistakes or poor choices of others affect us big time. The gambling scandal at Northwestern University during my residence as head coach—even though I was unaware of it at the time—affected our win/loss record that year and may have ultimately contributed to my being replaced. Sure I was hurt and disappointed. But what good would it have done to condemn those who were responsible? My challenge was how to retrieve that "miss" and turn it into an opportunity.

If you're a divorced mom and your "ex" doesn't show up when he's supposed to for his weekly visit with the kids, how do you respond? A significant person has dropped the ball, missed the shot—now what? Suppose, just suppose, you wait to find out what really happened before calling the kids' dad all sorts of names and accusing him of not caring about his kids. But suppose he really is a jerk—then what? Can you help salvage (and affirm) your kids' love for their dad even in the midst of a disappointment? Can you channel their disappointment into alternative activities that will help redeem the situation?

In an earlier chapter, I talked about the importance of teaching our children to "expect the unexpected" and to be able to handle it. That's what rebounding is all about. When one of your child's friends gossips about her behind her back, when a teacher promises to submit your child's essay in the city-wide creative writing contest and then forgets, when your daughter's "first love" dumps her abruptly for someone else, the challenge is to train our children to rebound and take the offensive.

Staying on the defensive would mean continuing to face the opponent, concentrating on the person (or team) who missed the shot—and miss any opportunity to rebound. Going on the offensive, on the other hand, would mean putting your opponent behind you ("boxing out"), so you can keep your eye on the ball or goal. The focus has shifted, and your child is in position to rebound.

When the other person who misses the shot is a "worthy opponent" (people we meet in the game of life—store clerks, teachers, neighbors, kids in school), the best offense is to keep our game plan clearly in mind and find a way to move forward. When the other person who misses the shot is someone on our own team (close friends and family), it might be tempting to chew him or her out for letting us down. But as any basketball player knows, it could have been one team member as easily as another—and next time it could be me.

I didn't learn about basketball in Sunday school, but I did learn that God cautions us to treat the person who makes a mistake with a certain humility, knowing full well it could be us next time. (See Galatians 6:1 in the Bible.) It works for basketball. It works for the game of life.

WHAT ABOUT WHEN WE (PARENTS) MISS THE SHOT?

I'm stretching the analogy here, but the fact is that in the game of life, we parents make our share of mistakes too. We lose our temper or we break a promise . . . 'fess up, it happens. A lot of parents don't want to admit to their kids that they make mistakes, because they're afraid it will weaken their authority.

Don't kid yourselves. Your kids already know you're not perfect. And believe it or not, they don't have a problem with that. What they *do* have a problem with, is when you can't admit your mistakes.

Parents, the mistakes you make are actually prime opportunities to model rebounding techniques. How you handle your own mistakes will make an indelible impression on your kids for how to handle their own "missed shots." Dad, maybe you've had a long day at work, you've battled snarled traffic for an hour on the way home, your nerves are shot, so the first thing you do when you step through the door is yell at the kids about all the toys they've left lying around. They run crying to their rooms.

Failure is only the opportunity to begin again, more intelligently.

—Henry Ford, auto manufacturer

If you don't do anything about it, it's going to be a "missed shot," without any opportunity to move your family team forward. But if you admit you were wrong, apologize to your wife and kids, ask their forgiveness, and start over, you've just accomplished two things. You've *retrieved a missed opportunity*, giving yourself another chance to score, and you've modeled how to turn a missed shot into a rebound.

Some of the mistakes parents make aren't so simple. Blind ambition, absence from the home, alcohol abuse, verbal or physical abuse, neglect, bitter fights—some families are in a sorry mess. But Dad, Mom, it's never too late to retrieve a missed opportunity. Admit it. Accept God's forgiveness. Forgive yourself. Ask forgiveness from those you've hurt. Seek help if you need it. Take the offensive to get your family in order.

It doesn't matter what the final score is. You'll be a winning team. Your kids might even vote you MVP.

FAILING TO REBOUND HAS CONSEQUENCES

1. *Some people let one missed shot throw off their whole game.* Ever hear one of your kids wail in adolescent angst, "My whole day is *ruined!*" Never mind that she went out to breakfast with Dad, got an A on her English paper, had twelve calls from friends after school. But somebody or something went wrong and it cast a dark cloud over everything that came before and after.

2. *Others are too humiliated (proud) to accept that they "missed,"* so they pretend that they weren't really trying for *that* goal and, of course, don't try again. If your kids are not able to own up to their misses, they won't be in position to seize a second chance—even as adults. What will they do if the first job interview goes bad, or they aren't chosen for the development team, or their prize manuscript comes back with a rejection slip? Will they walk away muttering, "Well, I didn't want it anyway"?

In relationships, if they are too embarrassed or ashamed to say, "I blew it. I'm sorry. Forgive me. I want to do better next time," they may not get a second chance.

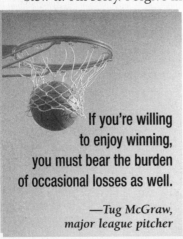

If you're willing to enjoy winning, you must bear the burden of occasional losses as well.

—*Tug McGraw, major league pitcher*

3. *Then there are those who just don't have the confidence to try something new.* They don't want to take risks, so they keep plodding along only doing what's "safe." What does it take to step out of your comfort zone and try something new? First, you have to believe that winning only comes after some failures along the way—provided we learn from them.

In our church, we like to say, "God is good—*all the time*" and "All the time—God is good." Does that mean that we never struggle with anything? That nothing bad ever happens? Of course not. I don't know about yours, but our church is full of ordinary people who have their share of challenges and struggles. But saying that God is good all the time is an expression of our faith that no matter what happens, we still have an awful lot to be thankful for. God does-n't change. He is still there for us, giving us the courage to keep press-ing on. It really changes our perspective—I know it has changed mine.

Wake up, parents! If we want our kids to achieve excellence, to develop all that God has put inside them, to be all they can be, we need to drill "Rebound! Rebound! Rebound!" into their daily life practices so that they're ready to retrieve those missed opportunities.

INSTANT REPLAY

Team confidence to rebound begins with the coaching staff. When my players bounce one off the rim, they know I'm not going to moan and turn away. I'm going to be looking for that rebound. When we're down ten points with only five minutes on the clock, they know I'm going to say, "Game ain't over yet." When the clock runs out and it's a loss? "There's going to be another game." There's *always* going to be another game.

As a parent coaching my kids in the game of life, I realize that my attitude toward mistakes and failures makes a big difference in how my kids are going to rebound. We parents sometimes get over-invested in our child's accomplishments. Sure we want them to be winners. But are we also willing to let them try and fail, get up and try again? Do I instill confidence in my daughters and son that a "missed shot" isn't the end of the game? Am I training them to retrieve those missed opportunities, learn from their mistakes, and turn them into victories?

It's important to keep our goals as a parent in mind. What do we most value for our children? Is it accolades and victory? Or character and perseverance?

A child who isn't afraid of failure, who is willing to learn from mis-takes, who doesn't let setbacks along the way knock her out of the game, who keeps a positive attitude about the future—that kind of child has all the earmarks of an MVP to me!

FREE THROW

1. When your child tries to do something and "misses the mark," how does he or she describe what happened? (Check all that apply.)

___ I'm stupid.	___ Stop pushing me!
___ I'll never be any good.	___ Well, at least I tried.
___ I knew I couldn't do it.	___ I know I could have done better.
___ I don't want to talk about it.	___ I'll do better next time.
___ So? What's the big deal?	___ I know where I made a mistake.
___ It's not my fault.	___ I want to try it again.
___ I didn't want to do it anyway.	___ I learned something.

2. Evaluate with your spouse or another parent how "rebounding practice" on your family team is going:

- I'm willing to admit my own mistakes.
- When I drop the ball, I'm willing to tell my children (or my spouse) "I'm sorry."
- I encourage my children to try new things, even if they're not especially good in that area.
- I applaud my children for "effort" as well as for "success."
- I encourage my children to take responsibility for their own actions and attitudes and not to blame things on others.
- I encourage my children not to give up.
- We talk through situations that don't work out well to see what can be learned.
- If my children use poor judgment, make a bad decision or a wrong choice, I let them know I believe they're capable of turning it around and doing the right thing.

11. HALF-TIME ADJUSTMENTS

After solid success in my first season at Northwestern, we had every reason to be optimistic. But to my disappointment, we encountered a slew of strategic injuries, among them center hopeful Evan Eschmeyer's foot injury and Nick Knapp's heart condition, and our team dropped to 5–22 in the 1994–95 season. At that time I didn't know that another reason for our poor showing was a gambling scandal in which two players conspired to throw key games. All I knew was that it was going to take me longer than I had left on my contract to rebuild a respectable team, so in the spring of 1996, I went to athletic director Rick Taylor and asked for an extension on my five-year contract.

Taylor said no; he would evaluate me at the end of the next season.

In terms of "keeping score," the next season (1996–97) did not go any better. It started off with star point guard Geno Carlisle transferring to California, claiming he was "tired of losing." Who could blame him or the others who bailed out or said no to our recruiting efforts?

Apparently Rick Taylor and the administration were also tired of losing. By the second week in February—just two-thirds of the way into the season—we were tied with Penn State for last place, staggering under a 6–16 record with only seven more games to play.

On Monday, the tenth, Rick Taylor called me into his office. There would be no extension. In fact, he fired me, one year before my contract expired.

A thousand protests and rejoinders ran through my mind, but what could I do? Finally I issued a statement simply acknowledging to the press that I had lost my job and quoting what was for me an encouraging verse from the Bible: "Consider it all joy, my brethren, when you encounter various trials; knowing that the testing of your faith produces endurance. And let endurance have its perfect result, that you may be perfect and complete, lacking in nothing."[1]

I called my wife, Sherialyn. The news was not entirely unexpected, because the local sports media had been hounding the Chicago area colleges to do something—*anything*—to bring home more victories. Still it was a shock that was going to require some major "half-time adjustments" for our family.

PREDICTABLE AND UNEXPECTED "HALF TIMES"

For sports teams, the break in the action afforded by half time is crucial for evaluating the effectiveness of the team's game plan and making any necessary adjustments. Coaches use it to refocus the team on their goals, renew the players' hope, and maintain their fighting spirit.

Sometimes other events trigger a similar time for major reevaluation. They might be injuries, a player quitting the team, or other unexpected crises.

In the family, both kinds of "half times" occur as well. If we don't recognize them, we are likely to try to play on through to our own detriment. In the family, we need breaks even more than an athletic team does. Sports teams go from game to game with lots of time for adjustments in between, but the family has to recognize the opportunities when they present themselves and make the most of half-time breaks. Like a good coach, you must be ready to make the right adjustments so that your kids can finish the game of life on top.

What constitutes these half-time breaks for the family? The following are some of the *predictable transitions*.

- the beginning of summer vacation
- the beginning of a new school year

---

[1]James 1:2-4, the Holy Bible

- the arrival of a new baby
- graduation to a new school
- the onset of puberty
- getting a driver's license
- starting to date

Half-time adjustments are just as important for the *unexpected crises*, such as:

- losing your job
- divorce
- a natural disaster
- the death of a family member
- a handicapping injury or illness
- a major rejection by a girlfriend or boyfriend

Whether prompted by predictable transitions or unexpected crises, these major adjustment times are not primarily the result of our kids' actions or choices. In large measure, they just happen. That is not to say that no one in the family bears any responsibility. Certainly my inability to lead the Wildcats to victory led to my dismissal; in most cases, both spouses bear some responsibility for a divorce. But as far as the kids are concerned, we aren't talking about their actions or choices in the same way as we talked about "rebounding from missed shots" in the last chapter.

We're looking at the big picture, the opportunities to make adjustments in the game plan. In light of this, there are certain important half-time tasks to consider.

1. Focus on the Mission

Whether it is a predictable transition or an unexpected crisis, our first response should be to remain focused on our mission. You may decide to adjust your game plan, but you don't want to panic and depart from your mission.

I nearly panicked after I was dismissed from Northwestern. The first thing I did was put our house up for sale. We had already lived in several cities while I pursued my coaching career. And because my only job experience to that point had been in coaching, I assumed that I needed another coaching job in another city—quick. I also found it hard to face people around town. In one interview, I said, "Evanston isn't a pleasant place to be these days. You've got to cut your ties and move on. That's the best thing to do."

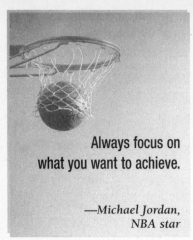

Always focus on what you want to achieve.

—*Michael Jordan, NBA star*

But none of those reasons for putting our house on the market had anything to do with our family mission statement. In fact, I hadn't even thought about our mission. I was on the verge of panic. The value of going back and focusing on your mission is to help you avoid panic, to see things in perspective, and to open your mind to all the alternatives before making rash decisions.

As I mentioned in chapter 1, the mission statement for our family was simply ". . . to make our world a better place by helping others to fulfill God's plan for their lives so that God will say to us when we see Him, 'Well done, my good and faithful servants.'" But it took a little time before I calmed down enough to consider how this applied to losing my job.

Focusing on your family mission or the mission statement you have for your children is helpful even when you're dealing with a less traumatic and more predictable transition, such as the beginning of a new school year. Suppose your mission statement for your kids included something like, "I don't want my children to expect other people to do for them what they can do for themselves." And you recall that last school year, mornings were a madhouse as you got your fourth, sixth, and ninth graders up and at it, made breakfast, packed lunches, made sure they all had their boots and coats on, and pushed them out the door to catch the bus before eight.

Focusing on your mission might help you to come up with a new plan requiring your children to take more responsibility in the morning. Maybe they can make their own lunches, lay out their clothes the night before, even help with breakfast. Maybe your ninth grader should take full responsibility for catching the bus. If he misses it, he walks—and is late.

Focusing on the mission can help bring things into perspective that might otherwise be distorted by guilt or fear or expedience or any number of other irrelevant factors.

2. Reiterate Your Expectations

In basketball, reiterating your expectations as a coach is always part of any half-time adjustment. In light of your mission, you've made plans and given specific instructions for how the team should play. Each man must do his job, but you notice that one of your men seems distracted. So at half time you confront him: "I told you to keep number 44 out of the key, but you're letting him have a picnic in there. If you don't do your job, someone else has to jump in, and that messes up our whole defense."

Going over specific expectations played a part in my personal crisis too. After putting our house on the market, I set about applying for several coaching positions that were open around the country. Responses were few, and I suddenly began to realize that there were not many athletic directors out there looking for a new coach they could announce as the guy who just got fired from Northwestern! Panic again gripped me.

Finally I got one solid offer—from Wyoming.

I might have accepted it if my wife hadn't reviewed some of the expectations we had for our family. Those expectations were more specific than a mission statement, and maybe that helped me to see that running off to Wyoming wasn't the right solution. She reminded me that we wanted to raise our children in a multi-cultural, multi-racial environment, where they would have the many advantages of urban life and be able to associate with other children like themselves. As a black family accustomed to big cities, the "Cowboy State" did not seem to fit our expectations.

Another expectation was for me—at age forty—not to take a step backward in my career path. Articulating that fact helped me to be clear (at least for the time being) that I shouldn't accept an assistant coach position after two tenures as a head coach.

We said no.

No matter what kind of transition you're going through, half times are good times to review family expectations. A lot of expectations in a family go uncommunicated; no wonder transitions are difficult! Even something as innocent and exciting as a family vacation can become a battleground if the various family members are operating with different expectations. If I say I want to leave "early" for the car trip to visit relatives in Atlanta, for example, I might be thinking 5:00 A.M., while my wife is thinking 8:30. That's why family half times are so valuable—to make sure everyone is on the same page, so that you can evaluate decisions and options with the same expectations.

As for my own job-hunting process, weeks went by with no other options. Then one day in late spring I called my friend Ray McCallum, the head coach at Ball State in Muncie, Indiana, just to see if he knew of any leads.

"Well," he said, "I've got an opening for an assistant on my staff if you'd be interested."

Interested? By this time we were realizing that we might not be able to meet all our expectations. And Coach McCallum was a good coach and a good friend. It was very tempting. "But," I said, "didn't I hear that another man has been hired for that position?"

"No, we haven't actually hired him yet," said Coach McCallum. "We talked, but we didn't finalize anything, so the job's yours if you want it."

This was wonderful. Of course, we weren't too excited about leaving all our friends and our church and our nice home and pulling the kids out of school before the end of the year, but, hey, beggars can't be choosers, right? We made plans to go down on a Monday to check out the schools, look for housing, and sign the contract. But on the proceeding Sunday, Norma Cox, a woman at our church, told my wife that we didn't need to be concerned about moving. She said she'd been praying for us. "God told me that He has something better for you," she said.

Sherialyn raised her eyebrows skeptically. But Norma said with a knowing look, "You'll see. I don't believe you'll be going anywhere."

No way, I thought, when Sherialyn told me about this conversation. This late in the spring, with no other coaching positions available, a bird in the hand was better than two in the bush, and I was going to take the job, backward career step or not.

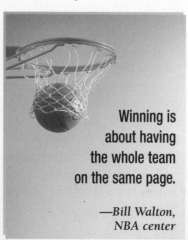

Winning is about having the whole team on the same page.

—*Bill Walton, NBA center*

But late Sunday night, the phone rang. It was Coach McCallum. He was terribly apologetic, but said there had been an awful mix-up. The original applicant thought he'd been given the position and had quit his other job. "I really feel like I ought to let him have it," said Coach McCallum. "I'm really sorry, Ricky, but he has cut all his ties and is literally on his way with his family right now."

Click. There went that option.

Then I thought about what Norma Cox had said. Maybe God *did* have something better. But in the meantime, what was I supposed to do to provide for my family?

3. Huddle the Team

The dynamics of my unexpected half-time crisis played itself out on two fronts: with my family (the need for a new job, the uncertainty of whether we were going to move, etc.) and with the Northwestern basketball team (what was going to happen to them for the seven remaining games?). After my dismissal was announced, several Wildcat players threatened to quit. They believed in me and in my coaching ability. They understood that I needed more time. I appreciated their loyalty, but quitting in protest wouldn't have done them any good. I intended to hold my head up high, but I didn't want to pour gasoline on the fire, so I looked for ways to keep the team together if at all possible. I worked out an arrangement with the administration to continue coaching the team through the season; this took some of the pressure off. But still the team was resentful. The team captain, Jevon Johnson, was issuing statements to the press like, "[Coach Byrdsong] did not get his chance."

I needed to diffuse the tension. Maybe a little humor would help.

After our game with Michigan State, I entered the post-game news conference holding a sign that read, "Will work for food!" The room broke up. A little later, in response to a reporter's question about what I was going to do next, I said, "I think I'm going to reapply for *this* job. I can't imagine anyone else wanting it!" At another interview, I quipped, "My life's got to be easier from this point on. Hey, you can't keep having as much bad luck as I've had."

A little levity seemed to help. The guys rallied round, and we finished the season together.

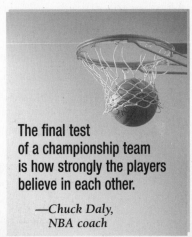

Of course, my personal family needed attention too. My daughter Sabrina said, "Daddy, what does 'fired' mean?" Not an easy question. I knew it was nothing personal with Rick Taylor; the university was just looking at the bottom line. After I tried to explain, she stuck me with another: "You going to keep trying to coach?"

"Yes, I am."

The final test of a championship team is how strongly the players believe in each other.

—*Chuck Daly, NBA coach*

"Are you going to try to be a football coach?"

"Football coach? Why would I try being a football coach?"

"Because they win. Their games are easier."

Yes, well, at that point Northwestern football coach Gary Barnett was having fine success on the gridiron. But the conversation pointed up how personally children take our struggles. Don't ever presume that they understand it all and don't need some special support. Calling for a family huddle will give everyone the extra affirmation they need.

When your family enters a half-time break—especially if it results from an unexpected crisis—there may be "players" who are so distraught that they don't even know whether there is a team anymore, let alone whether they are a part of it. You need to take the time and effort to keep the family together and to affirm every child's participation and importance. Don't take anything for granted.

If your family faces a serious crisis such as divorce or death, be sure to seek counseling. Even older children can subconsciously think that they are the cause of a divorce or someone's death. It is important to not let the team disintegrate because of such events.

4. Take a Break From the Action

The season was over, and I was out of a job. As a family, we had rallied together and affirmed that we were still a team and everyone was important. We had reviewed our mission, but still there was no job. It was too late to find another coaching job for the following season. I had faced some of my limitations, the most obvious being that I had never worked at anything other than coaching. I had no other experience, no other easily marketable skills. Maybe I needed to take a big break and gain some new training.

In the context of a game, one of the important things that happens at half time is that everyone gets to take a break from the action, catch their breath, and drink some fluids to replenish electrolytes. Rather than continuing to butt my head against the wall, I decided I needed a break.

I had a lot of ideas bouncing around in my head and a desire to share them with other people. Coaching had taught me a lot about life and relationships—even parenting! Maybe I should write a book. So I started making notes. Writing became my break. Everyone used to joke about my yellow pad and purple pen. I took them everywhere with me, jotting down ideas whenever they popped into my head. Then I realized that this was getting serious. I found a little office space at our church, The Worship Center, and every day I'd go there and write, just like I was going to work.

In time I began to view my writing *as* my work. I knew that I was a good motivational speaker, and I imagined that my new game plan might include writing a book or two and going on the speaking circuit.

What kinds of breaks might fit you and your family? Some predictable transitions, like entering junior high or getting a driver's license, can benefit from a family meeting and taking time out to discuss new privileges and responsibilities. Some transitions (like graduation) deserve a celebration, maybe a special party or a meal out together. A lot of children entering puberty have benefited from a weekend away with the same-sex parent to discuss the meaning, implications, and moral challenges that will come with the teen years. It can be a wonderful bonding time that not only provides guidance but opens communication on a subject far too many families leave solely to the public schools.

5. Evaluate and Adjust the Game Plan

One of the advantages of taking a break from the action is the opportunity to evaluate and adjust the game plan. Some family transitions—your teen gets his driver's license or starts dating—even though normal and predictable, need new strategies of "offense" and "defense." And many unpredictable transitions—a job that requires more travel away from home, a major illness, or the loss of a parent to death or divorce—demand major adjustments to the family game plan. If you don't take time to evaluate what's needed, the family team can slide into chaos.

For me, the break from the nonstop action of coaching and searching for a job allowed me to evaluate and adjust my game plan. I realized that one of my greatest strengths was coaching young people in the game of life. Even after I was fired, a lot of my players said, "He cared about us as people." That comment made me feel good. They got the message: The game isn't just about the final score.

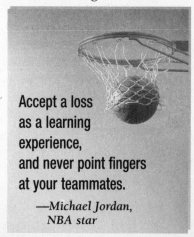

Accept a loss as a learning experience, and never point fingers at your teammates.
—*Michael Jordan, NBA star*

Months went by. Fortunately we were not yet facing a financial crisis since I was still getting paid for the last year of my five-year contract. But I wasn't working, and I needed to look to the future.

One day I decided to approach Patrick Ryan, chairman and chief executive of the Aon Corporation. He was also the chairman of the board of trustees at Northwestern University, and in that capacity had known and supported me as Northwestern's basketball coach. Possibly, with his many connections, he could help me get my book published.

I went to see him on September 24, seven months after I had been fired from Northwestern. What happened in that meeting exceeded all my expectations.

When I came out of that interview, I had a revised game plan, one that fit me even better.

BEGINNING THE SECOND HALF

I found a phone and called Sherialyn. "It's over!"

"What's over?" she said.

"The waiting is over. You're not going to believe this."

"What did Pat say?"

"He said that he liked my idea for a book. Not only is he going to help me with the book but he also offered me a job with Aon while I'm writing it. You're talking to the new vice president of community affairs for the Aon Corporation!"

The job involved representing Aon at corporate functions throughout Chicagoland, but—I could hardly contain my excitement—my *primary* responsibilities would be developing programs to help underprivileged youth reach their full potential. I would get to "coach" young people through various programs all across the country and do motivational speaking to both children and adults. And I'd also have time to write.

Sherialyn was just as astounded and pleased as I was. We both knew what this meant: We wouldn't have to sell the house, we wouldn't have to move, we wouldn't have to uproot the kids, and I'd be doing what I have always loved to do—coaching young people in the game of life.

My half time was over. It was time to get back in the game.

For me, all five elements had taken place. They may not have happened in order—I'm not sure the order matters much—and my faith had been sorely tested. But I had (1) regained focus on the mission, (2) reiterated our expectations, (3) affirmed that our family was a team, (4) taken a break from the action, and (5) evaluated and adjusted my game plan. I was ready for my second half.

CREATING AN "INTERVENTION" HALF TIME

So far we have discussed two types of half times: predictable transitions and unexpected crises. But there actually is a third type of half time that is neither natural nor unexpected. It is a half-time experience that you calculate to be needed and then create. One might call it an "intervention."

In sports, these would be analogous to time-outs, though the short duration of a time-out would seldom allow for the five steps we've identified as useful for a half-time adjustment. In the family, however, there are times when as parents we need to call a halt to business as usual, we need to intervene in the way our kids are going. We need to *create* a half time where none exists so that we can focus on the mission, reiterate expectations, affirm our team solidarity, evaluate and encourage our players, and adjust the game plan. Maybe we want to grab our kids' attention, shake them up a little so they'll face reality, or break old patterns and influences.

The need for a half-time intervention might range from something fairly minor—like the realization that your kids have gotten into the pattern of watching too much TV—to a major concern such as gang involvement or alcohol abuse. Whether big or small, you will undoubtedly encounter a time when you need to bring life-as-usual to a halt in order to "get some things straight" and make a half-time adjustment.

For instance, a few years ago it was customary in Evanston for high school seniors to spend all night in hotel rooms after the prom. One father had heard that wild kids went to wild parties, but he had no idea "everybody" was doing it until his son announced his plans to rent a hotel room with some friends. "We're not going to drink or have sex," his son hastened to assure him. "We just want to have a good time."

"Over my dead body," said his father. "I believe that you don't *intend* it to be a night of drinking and sex, but it's a problem waiting to happen."

A line had been drawn in the sand—a serious challenge for an eighteen-year-old who thought it was time to be emancipated! What saved the day was an "intervention," where the parents and the youth sat down and went through several of the half-time steps until they came up with an acceptable alternative. To begin with, the parents agreed that it wasn't their mission (or desire) to be killjoys or to embarrass their son with his peers. There were, however, certain expectations that still stood while he was part of the family. They then had to take a break to do some creative brainstorming before they came up with an adjustment that worked.

Their solution was to arrange for an uncle with a large sailboat to take three couples out for a supervised moonlight cruise and sunrise breakfast on Lake Michigan. When word of these plans got out, several other seniors begged for a place on the boat. The parents had devised a wholesome plan to "out-party" the hotel revelers. Within a couple years the high school itself began scheduling a cruise boat for post-prom festivities.

As parents, we sometimes do need to do something unusual to intervene when things are going in the wrong direction and no traditional corrective works. Here are a few other half-time interventions that parents have successfully employed.

- Some families, when they have seen that their children need more attention, have downsized their wage earners by bringing a parent home. Either Dad has cut out all the overtime or Mom has decided to become a stay-at-home mom. It is a costly choice, but usually not impossible. Kids seldom *need* more money, but they often need more of you.

- More and more families have chosen to homeschool their kids. Some choose this as their long-term educational strategy. Others have switched to it for a couple of years—as we did. Either way, it is a big sacrifice, but if the children need it, it can be very worthwhile.

- Some families have gone on long summer car trips in order to spend extended time together to cement relationships with growing children or to break into patterns not otherwise accessible. A leave of absence from one's job or pulling from the savings account can be very costly—but you'd be surprised what you can do if you really decide it is necessary. And if it is necessary, the results are worth far more than that new SUV you've been eyeing.

- Occasionally sending an older kid out of town for an extended period to a trustworthy relative or a well-run summer camp can help. It can give a kid the chance to break out of some bad patterns or relationships and grow up a little bit. But it can also be risky. Three cautions: (1) Make sure the child does not think you are trying to get him or her "out of your hair." (2) Make sure the new setting will be better than the present one or the problem will duplicate itself. (3) Try to solicit the child's cooperation in using this as an occasion to change for the better.

- Move the whole family! This may be the most drastic and costly, but there are situations where so many influences in a child's life—peers, neighborhood, school, police—all are so negative and so overwhelming that a child would have to be Samson to break free. This is sometimes true for kids involved with gangs. Their reputation makes it almost impossible for them to get out, not primarily because of the pressure from other gang members, real as that can be, but also because of the negative expectations of teachers and police and other kids not in the gang. Everyone expects the worst. One caution: There is almost no high school in the country free from gang or gang-like activity. Do your research (with the police, schools, and park districts). At least make sure the old gang or its primary rivals are not present in the new setting. A move provides an opportunity, but your child will only change if he or she *wants* to change.

Of course, not all interventions need to be so drastic. Intentionally breaking into any unacceptable pattern could be called an intervention if you embark on it in the half-time format. One key to the success of this kind of half-time adjustment with your kids is your willingness to give more of yourself. Many interventions require something more from you, either more of your time, closer supervision, or some other creative investment. (Throwing money at a problem without investing yourself seldom does any good.) Even if some of your specific techniques don't work, if you give of yourself and your time, your kids will realize your love and commitment to them, and they may be more likely to respond.

INSTANT REPLAY

The three half times we have discussed produce different reactions. Predictable transitions are usually welcomed. Unexpected crises are often dreaded. And essential interventions can sometimes be costly.

Like the standard half time in a basketball game, when everyone gets a chance to take a much-needed breather, down some liquids, and wipe the sweat out of their eyes, kids usually look forward to the *predictable transitions* in their own lives—graduating from elementary or middle school, getting a driver's license, or going on that first date. Of course there is some trepidation in these transitions, but it is usually overcome with eagerness. In fact, the eagerness may eclipse the need for evaluation and adjustment. Hey, why not just kick back and spend the whole half time drinking Gatorade and patting each other on the back? But there's work to do even if things are going well. There will be new challenges, and you need to prepare for them.

No one, however, welcomes *unexpected crises*. We try to prevent them; we try to postpone them; when they strike, we sometimes deny their reality or magnitude. Nevertheless, the emergencies they engender have their way of demanding our attention. The question is, will we attend to the steps required for an effective half time, or will we panic and do something foolish?

Interventions may be tempting when you think everything is going awry, but if you have not counted the cost and realized that you may have to invest yourself more sacrificially in your kids, then you may be deceiving yourself. Intervention should not be a self-indulgent tantrum to express your personal frustration, but rather a constructive half time designed to really give your child a new opportunity.

Whatever transition your family is facing, whether minor or major, the half-time break offers an opportunity to be *pro*active rather than *re*active.

FREE THROW

Photocopy the next two pages for each of your children. After writing a child's name on each sheet, identify and circle whether he or she is facing a *predictable transition*, is in the middle of an *unexpected crisis*, or needs a *calculated intervention*. Then, on the right hand side of the first line, name what that half-time event is. Finally, develop plans for each step in your half-time adjustment for that child.

If you have concluded that your child needs some type of intervention, use a separate sheet of paper to describe the risks and how you will invest yourself more fully in that's child's life. Consider whether you need professional advice before initiating any intervention.

Plans for Half Time

Child's Name:_____Transition/Crisis/Intervention Event_____

1. *Focus on the mission.*
   Review your Family Mission Statement from chapter 1, number 2
   under Free Throw. Write here any personalized or additional elements for this child.

2. *Reiterate your expectations.*
   In the pursuit of your mission, what specifics do you expect to
   remain constant?

3. *Affirm team solidarity.*
   What elements in this event may threaten your family unity?

   What can you do to counteract that threat? How can you assure your
   child that he or she is a valued part of the team? Be specific.

4. *Take a break from the action.*

Decide how and where you can commemorate this event. The beginning of summer or the school year might merit a sit-down meeting. Graduation, possibly a special dinner out. Approaching puberty, maybe a weekend away with the same-sex parent to discuss how to handle the moral challenges ahead.

5. *Evaluate and adjust the game plan.*

Be specific in deciding how your game plan needs to change in response to this event. Don't forget, each step of additional maturity should be accompanied by new privileges and new responsibilities.

12. PLAYIN' ON THROUGH

In 1997, when the Chicago Bulls were contending with the Utah Jazz for a fifth NBA title, the Bulls went into Game Five with two wins at the United Center, two losses in Utah, and one game to go in Utah before the two teams returned to Chicago. Utah hadn't lost a home game for twenty-three straight games, so the Jazz went into Game Five with a huge home-court advantage, not to mention the momentum of winning the last two games.

As if that wasn't bad enough, Michael Jordan was sick. Not runny-nose sick. Horrible stomach-virus sick. In fact, an hour before game time, he was so sick his teammates wondered if he had the energy to suit up, much less play.

No one would have blamed Jordan if he sat it out even though without him the Bulls probably would have headed home to Chicago behind 2–3. But hey, if you're sick, you're sick. After all, basketball players are human, just like the rest of us.

But Michael Jordan not only knows how to ride the crest of success, he also knows how to play on through—and that's what he did that night. "It [would have been] easy to sit back and say, 'I've given my best,

I'm tired, somebody else has got to do it,'" said Jordan later. "I didn't take that approach. I thought positive and did whatever I could do, gave every little inch of energy that I had." By game's end, Jordan had scored 38 of his team's final tally and hit a huge three-pointer with only 25 seconds left, which gave the Bulls the lead, before he collapsed into Scottie Pippen's arms. The Jazz clawed back with a bucket and a free throw, but Jordan had to trust his teammates to hang on to the lead he had given them and win, 90–88.

What a game! It was a beautiful example of why Michael Jordan is an extraordinary athlete. He reached down deep into himself to overcome some huge obstacles that night. He had faith in his teammates. And he never gave up.

Jordan personifies the fundamental attitude of a winner: "Refuse to lose! Keep playin' on through!" No matter how many times he was down, he always came up fighting.

PLAYING FROM BEHIND

Every coach has had the awful feeling of being behind in the game. At times there can be no worse feeling, because all the planning and preparation was intended to prevent this from happening. And make no mistake, the players are going to feel discouraged too. There are a lot of factors that can put a team "behind": losing the previous game, fatigue, loss of a key player to an injury or illness, playing against a stronger opponent who is "expected" to win, or simply being down in the score late in the game.

Refuse to lose!

—John Calipari,
NBA and college coach

This is a critical situation. It's easy to keep the momentum going when you've got a twenty-point lead. But to play from behind, a team must draw on their preparation, perseverance, and perspective ("hustle and heart") in order to play on through.

What does it mean to "play from behind" when we're talking about the family?

First of all, how do you know if you are behind? What is your measurement standard? Are you comparing your first child to your second? Comparing your child to someone else's kid? Comparing your family to the one who just won the lottery? Family goals based on the strengths and potential of the individual members of your own family team are a far more accurate measurement of the ability to come out "winners" than simply comparing your children or your family to someone else.

And don't assume you're behind just because you lack certain resources. It's tempting for a neighborhood team to moan that they don't have any funding to get uniforms ("We're at a disadvantage to start with!"), but a lot of dynamic playing takes place on asphalt courts in mismatched sweats and T-shirts. On the other hand, a bunch of basketball hopefuls can name themselves the Rockin' Rockets and brag about their fancy uniforms and all-star talent all they want, but unless they set a goal and get themselves out on the court to play the game, it doesn't mean much.

The point is, a family on a limited income is not automatically "behind," and a family with money to spare is not automatically "ahead" in the game of life. Winning is related to the goals we have set and are endeavoring to accomplish.

If you determine that you are, indeed, "playing from behind" in relation to the goals you've set, at least you know what your goals are! That's good news! And there isn't a sports team on earth that wins all its games. At one point or another (quite often, actually), a team must play from behind. The same is true of the family. If you have a mission statement for your family, and you have set goals for your children, reaching those goals will be a process of trial and error, learning from mistakes, learning from experience, rebounding from a setback, adjusting your game plan. In other words, playing from behind is a normal part of the process of *playing on through*.

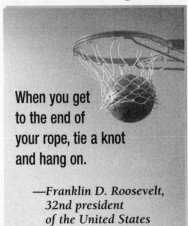

When you get to the end of your rope, tie a knot and hang on.

—*Franklin D. Roosevelt,*
32nd president
of the United States

When a team is playing from behind—for whatever reason—it helps to take your eyes off the final score, break down your game plan into a manageable goal, and focus on the present task. In other words, a team that is playing from behind catches up *one basket at a time*. Here are some ways to come up from behind.

Redefine the Terms of Success

Frequently when a coach knows that the opposition team outperforms his team in a certain area, he will *redefine the terms of success*. In other words, if Team A is dynamite at rebounding, with a habit of out-rebounding their opponents by 15, the coach of Team B might strategize: "Our goal is to rebound evenly with them." If they narrow that average in one game to 10, and in another game to 4, *that's success!*

A team like Duke University, which has a reputation for a strong defensive strategy, might use a half-court trap to force the team with possession into a weak pass that Duke can intercept and turn into a fast-break lay-up. Six turnovers like that and—voilà! Twelve points. But a wise coach, whose team is playing from behind, might say, "Our goal is to limit Duke to two fast-break lay-ups instead of six."

A family in our church took on the task of being foster parents to an "at risk" teenager. I'll call her Suzi. Her birth mom—a single parent—didn't speak English, so Suzi had no help with homework and was falling behind in school. She was socially promoted by an irresponsible school system, but by the time Suzi reached the ninth grade she was failing, and spent more time hanging out on the street with questionable friends than in class. Her mother had already kicked her out of the house and gladly accepted the offer of a foster home.

When Suzi went to live with her new family, they had one condition. She had to attend school *every day*. Suzi agreed, though it wasn't easy. There were a lot of mornings when she felt like ditching. But she knew if she quit school, it was back to her mom's, and that wasn't a good scene. At the end of the first semester, Suzi's grades were still pretty dismal—but she had perfect attendance! Her foster parents took her out to dinner to celebrate. Suzi had reached her first goal.

Reinforce the Team Concept

In Suzi's case, it took a youth pastor who believed Suzi wasn't a lost cause, her foster parents who encouraged her, a foster brother in college who was willing to give up his room "to come home to," a foster sister who was willing to share the bathroom, concerned teachers and social workers at school, and Suzi herself to work toward the goal: graduation from high school. When Suzi walked down the aisle four years later in cap and gown, the whole team was there to cheer.

When you're playing from behind—or even if you've simply got a long season ahead with the normal wins and losses—it's important to *reinforce the team concept of all being in the game together* for the long haul. When one player is strengthened, the whole team is strengthened.

Remain Confident in Your Team's Ability to Win

While I was writing this book, Loyola University's Ramblers and their new basketball coach, Larry Farmer, were struggling. They lost the first game of the season to Wisconsin, a humiliating 66–29. Then, just when it looked like the Ramblers were turning a corner with back-to-back home victories against Midwestern Collegiate Conference opponents, they fell behind again with three straight losses—the last of which was an embarrassing 19-point deficit on their home court.

Still, Farmer was optimistic. "I've told [my team] I never get to the point where I give up on them and that this is not an off year or a rebuilding year," he said. "This is a year we're going to do as well as we can and try to win our conference and our conference tournament and get to the NCAA tournament."[1]

At the same time Farmer was planning ahead, scheduling the opponents he thought his team would be ready for the following year and the year after that.

Good coaches understand that they must continue to have hope that things will turn around. And that hope must reflect itself in the passion with which they continue to coach. If the *coach remains confident in the team's ability to win*, the players will feel this confidence and won't lose heart when things don't go as well as expected.

> The man who wins may have been counted out several times, but he didn't hear the referee.
>
> —*H. E. Jansen,*
> *American author*

Parents, this is what it means to believe in our children. Not that our kids won't make mistakes or hit rough spots. (Hey, we adults do too.) Sure there are disappointments. A poor report card, a call from the principal that says our child was caught cheating, a rebellious teen—those setbacks are rough. But *don't get sloppy with details just because there is no immediate payoff.* All the things we've talked about up to this point—unity and loyalty between husband and wife, commitment to the family, teaching kids the fundamental skills of success, consistency

---

[1]Tony Ginnetti, Staff Reporter. "A Rough Ramble," *Chicago Sun-Times*, Friday, January 15, 1999, 115.

in our discipline, knowing when to make adjustments in our game plan—these kinds of building blocks give our kids the resources for playing on through in spite of setbacks or losses.

Even when a coach knows that his team is too far down to win a specific game, it is critical that the team not quit. Playing on through is important preparation for the next game. As I said earlier, gaining even a little momentum will carry over! If a team can come from thirty points down at the half to end the game at only twelve down, that team has won an important victory, even if that game is lost. The final score is not the only factor to be considered. Improvement in the game is a victory in itself.

Losing the battle is not losing the war.

That's why it's so important for families to hang together through the ups and downs, through thick and thin, through good times and bad. There's always hope. And if we don't give our kids what they need to win in the game of life, who will?

If we keep the big picture in mind and if we know what we're reaching for, we can *remain focused on how to win, not on the fact that we're behind.*

Time Is on Our Side

What's great about the game of life is that it isn't over in forty minutes. The game of life isn't even over in a season. A college athletic coach has roughly four years to build a team. When the freshmen players come in, a lot of time is spent making them feel welcome, bonding as part of the team, seeing that their essential needs are met, evaluating their strengths and weaknesses. The sophomore year is spent working hard to learn fundamental skills and to incorporate all the information they're learning. In the junior year, the emphasis is on using their skills for the benefit of the team. The senior year is payoff time; we have an experienced team. But seasoned players are graduating all the time, requiring every year to be a *new start* of sorts.

But in coaching our kids, time is on our side.

God had a good idea, giving a baby nine months in the "cooker." Parents need that much time just to get ready! And even then, a lot of us aren't ready. Why don't babies come with instruction manuals? We buy a car, a microwave, even a can opener, and they all come with an instruction manual. You want to be a lawyer or a doctor? You spend a zillion years in school and *then* you have to pass the bar exam or spend a year as a resident, "practicing" medicine. But new parents are merely slapped on the back, given a few "Congratulations!" and somehow expected to raise children to become happy, productive human beings.

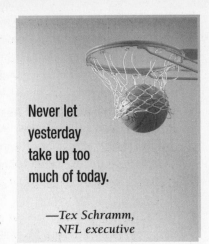

Never let yesterday take up too much of today.

—Tex Schramm, NFL executive

Maybe you're feeling discouraged right now. Your dad wasn't around when you were growing up, or you had an alcoholic parent, or you didn't have good role models of a healthy marriage. Your own family seems to be falling behind in the game of life. Maybe you've already suffered the setback of a divorce. You want your kids to be winners, but they seem to be making all the same mistakes you did.

It's not too late. The game isn't over yet. Time is on your side.

Maybe this book has given you a vision for the kind of family life you'd like to have. You haven't been the "family coach" you'd like to be, but you're willing to reset your priorities. This book doesn't have all the answers, but it can be a beginning. Reread it with your spouse or a friend. Talk to your pastor or priest or rabbi. Get some counseling. Attend a marriage or parenting seminar. Admit your mistakes to your family, learn to give and receive forgiveness, and play on through.

Work Yourself Out of a Job

Time has another benefit. It gives us a cushion to prepare our kids to play the game of life like a "pro," without Coach Mom or Coach Dad there calling every play.

"What's the big deal?" you say. "Doesn't it just happen? My baby eventually grows up and at eighteen goes off to college or gets a job, leaving me, finally, with an empty nest. Right?"

Not always. Sometimes those babies come back home—sponging off Mom and Dad ("Say, Pops, can I borrow fifty bucks?"), or you end up raising the grandkids because *your* kids never learned how to be responsible.

Or maybe *you* are the one who's having a hard time letting go. You're still washing and ironing clothes for your fifteen-year-old. You make all the decisions, you call all the plays, you pick up all the pieces.

Uh-uh. Part of the big picture in parenting is realizing that *you need to work yourself out of a job.* The goal of the game is to launch our kids to live on their own. But it doesn't happen overnight.

In one sense, the years spent in the home are like the time a team spends practicing before the season opens. As the first game of the season looms into view, a basketball coach will step up the pace. We start out doing run-throughs of a triangle defense or a full-court press at a slow pace until the players get the hang of it. As time for the game draws closer, we step up the pace, even beyond what the team might have to face during actual play. And, of course, preseason games give

This is what I'd been striving for ever since I started coaching: to become an "invisible" leader.

—*Phil Jackson,*
NBA coach

them a feel for how to put it all together. It has to be second nature, because you can never be sure what you will actually face on the court.

Parents should be doing a similar thing in the family. As you get closer to the time when your kids will run out onto the court of life, you step up the pace. You give your teenagers more responsibility and more opportunities to make decisions—and experience the consequences of those decisions. Maybe you decide they should handle all the money for their personal expenses. You might sit down with your teen and agree on a dollar amount he or she needs for bus fare, school lunches, clothing, and other necessities. Or you might agree that they need to earn their own money for clothing and "extras" such as movies or CDs with an after-school job, in which case you no longer provide spending money. If the latter is the case, your teen becomes responsible for managing his or her budget. If she spends it all on a "fabulous jacket," don't run to her rescue when she needs underwear.

One reason parents "overcoach" (see chapter 9) is that they don't have the perspective of working themselves out of a job and releasing their kids to make it on their own. It's a big mistake to try to tightly control everything in our kids' lives until they are eighteen or twenty-one and then think they are going to automatically succeed. If they don't rebel big-time before then, they'll crash when they're on their own.

The key is giving them increasing autonomy as they demonstrate increasing responsibility so that by the time they are out of the nest, they can live wisely and successfully without a lot of coaching from Mom and

Dad. And if you have deliberately and consistently been giving new responsibilities and privileges as your kids get older, you can counter complaints that "You *never* let me do anything!" by pointing to the steps you have already taken to help them become more self-sufficient.

Friends of ours with teenagers said they made a specific plan for weekend curfews that would increase throughout the high school years. Ninth grade curfew was 11:00. Tenth grade curfew was 11:30. Junior year was midnight. Senior year was 12:30. Exceptions were allowed when the situation warranted it and plans were made in advance. If their teens violated their curfew without a valid reason (and a phone call), they were bumped back to the *previous* curfew for a few weeks until they showed responsibility. The dad told us,

> It wasn't easy. Many of their friends had later curfews or no curfews at all. We were influenced by a street chaplain who reminded us, "Nothing positive happens after midnight." And for the most part, our kids respected their curfews and gave us phone calls if they were unavoidably late or wanted an extension. When our oldest graduated from high school—but before she left for college—we told her she could set her own curfew, meaning all we asked was that she let us know when she planned to come in and who she was with and what she was doing, which is no different than my wife and I do for each other. That's just common courtesy when you're living under the same roof.

"Working yourself out of a job" doesn't mean a parent has no rules or sets no limits. As long as your children are under your roof, you are responsible for them. And parents should *always* be available to support, talk through issues, give options, even point out consequences of certain choices. But even the rules and limits should gradually be replaced by *personal responsibility*, a *realistic* idea of what it means to be responsible.

Time away from the family can provide some of these learning experiences as well. Encouraging your older child to work for two to six weeks at a summer camp (as a counselor or even washing dishes), go on a trip with relatives, volunteer at a local animal shelter or hospital or soup kitchen, or get an after-school job all contribute to the experience of handling responsibility without Coach Mom or Coach Dad looking over his or her shoulder.

The point is, enjoying our children isn't an end in itself—although I'll be the first to admit I love those tickling sessions, playing in the park, and rooting for my kids at their basketball or soccer games. And I'm as proud as the next parent when one of my kids wins an award or gets an A on a report card or when someone says to me, "Your daughters are growing up to be fine young ladies." But my *job* as a parent is to prepare them for *playing on through* in the game of life with the courage to face life's ups and downs when their only "coach" is their conscience and God. And the only way I can do that is to work myself out of a job by gradually letting them go.

THE GAME IS NEVER OVER!

Now what I'm going to say may seem like a contradiction to "working ourselves out of a job."

We never stop being a parent. Our job description will change when our children move into adulthood—we will no longer be the hands-on "coach," responsible for shaping the family team—but we will still have a job to do as parents of adult children: to be the fan in the stands, giving emotional and spiritual support to our players, who eventually will become coaches to their own family teams. Some parents of adult children have told me they are enjoying their children in a new way—not as "peers," but with the kind of rich friendship that can extend across generations, built on mutual respect and love for one another.

One "empty nest" mom told me, "Five years ago my teenager considered any advice I gave as hopelessly old-fashioned and out-of-touch. Now she's calling me on the phone wanting to know how I manage my time schedule."

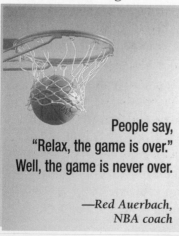

People say, "Relax, the game is over." Well, the game is never over.

—*Red Auerbach, NBA coach*

If we live our lives with integrity and establish a strong, loving relationship with our children, as adults they will turn to us for counsel—just as I turned to my former head coaches for support and advice when I took on my first head coaching job. And my guess is, as parents of grown kids, we will still hurt when they hurt, shout with excitement when they get that promotion, lose sleep when they're in danger or in trouble, and brag when they do well. In that sense, we never stop being a parent.

And the next stage, of course, is becoming grandparents! Traditionally in the black community, grandparents (and the extended family in general) have played an important role in the lives of the children. Depending on the family situation, Grandma might care for the kids while Mama works, or Grandpa might live with the family after Grandma dies, providing a wealth of intergenerational support. But today, given our highly mobile society, many grandparents live hundreds of miles away in another state. It takes a lot of dedication for grandparents and grandchildren to remain intimately involved across the miles—but it's not impossible! Phone calls, e-mail, and regular visits help keep the relationship active.

A new grandmother in our church said, "Grandparenting is one of the world's best kept secrets! I used to play 'house' when I was a little girl and I dreamed of being a mommy some day. But I never played 'grandma.' I had no idea it would be so exciting to develop a relationship with my children's children."

Whether they're next door or retired in Florida, grandparents are *family*. They are (or should be) an important part of the family "coaching staff." And there are many benefits grandparents can provide: wisdom for important decisions, experience in handling difficult situations, support and stability during rocky times, time to lend a listening ear, laughter at preschool jokes, unconditional love that's always present, and prayer to see you through.

In an earlier chapter, I told a story about a young woman in college who was strengthened by the knowledge that her father got up early every morning to pray for each of his kids by name. When she and her siblings got married, that father simply lengthened his prayer time to include the grandchildren that came, one after another. One grandchild in particular got in a lot of difficulty: alcohol and drug addiction and scrapes with the law. Every morning in the early hours this grandfather faithfully prayed. When he died, his daughter wondered, *Who is going to pray so faithfully for the grandchildren now?* She decided *she* needed to begin praying for her nieces and nephews regularly.

This brings up perhaps the most important point of all about "playin' on through" in the game of life.

RAISING CHILDREN IS A SPIRITUAL ACTIVITY WITH ETERNAL CONSEQUENCES

Sherialyn and I believe that passing on our faith is far more important than passing on any earthly inheritance. The Scriptures ask, "What good does it benefit a man [or woman] to gain the whole world, yet lose his soul?"[2] Playin' on through involves preparing your children for their eternal destiny.

Both the Jewish and Christian Scriptures give these instructions to parents: "These commandments that I give you today are to be upon your hearts. *Impress them on your children.* Talk about them when you sit at home and when you walk along the road, when you lie down and when you get up. Tie them as symbols on your hands and bind them on your foreheads. Write them on the doorframes of your houses and on your gates"[3] We have not equipped our children to "play on through" until we have *impressed* upon them the importance of their relationship with God.

Many times during the parenting process, the most effective way to "get in position to score" is on our knees in prayer. Sherialyn and I find wisdom for the challenges of raising our children by praying *for* them. We want to be the best parents we can possibly be, but we also know we aren't perfect. We need God's help and God's wisdom. Many times God leads us to pray *with* them. In this way, we share in their lives and day-to-day situations and demonstrate to them the importance of prayer.

In this and other crucial ways, *our parenting affects future generations.* Just as some of the players that I've coached have gone on to play on

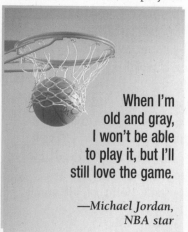

When I'm old and gray, I won't be able to play it, but I'll still love the game.

—*Michael Jordan, NBA star*

NBA teams or become coaches themselves, the way I parent my children will affect my grandchildren and their children after that. I'm not just training my children to be players in the game of life, but someday they will have the privilege of coaching their own family team. What kind of skills, values, and priorities will they be taking with them into *that* season of play?

Many families today are living in chaotic or dysfunctional family systems. *We can break the cycle of dysfunction and*

---

[2]Mark 8:36, the Holy Bible.

[3]Deuteronomy 6:6-9, the Holy Bible (italics added).

build healthy families. But it will take a commitment to *playin' on through.* My strong and earnest desire is that each mom or dad reading this book will show diligence and sincerity, the capacity to hang in there for the long haul, as you coach your kids in the game of life.

Remember, in this game, they can't afford to lose.

INSTANT REPLAY

What if we could instill this attitude in all our children: "Play on through! Refuse to lose!"

There are a lot of discouraged young people out there. They don't think they can make it. They're not doing well in school. They didn't make the team. They have very few skills. Their talents are undeveloped and untapped. They don't have family support. Society has given up on them. The most successful role models and "businessmen" in their community are the drug dealers who rake in thousands of dollars in a week. (What chance does flipping burgers for minimum wage have against *that*?) The future? They don't think about it. Too many of their peers will end up addicted, in jail, or dead.

But don't tell me we can't save the children. We save the children in the game of life just like we play from behind in a game of basketball—we catch up, one child at a time. We start in our own families, with our own children. Our passion for coaching our kids never falters until the last buzzer. And it doesn't stop there, because our kids take over and coach *their* kids, and we have the opportunity to sit in the stands and be their number one fans.

What about the other kids, the kids whose parents are too busy, or too stressed, or too lazy, or too successful, or "not there," or simply trying to parent alone?

Those kids need a Coach Lester, a man or a woman who will call them out and say, "Hey, son! Hey, young lady! Yes, *you*. You can do it! I'm gonna help you. Be there!"

You can be that coach.

FREE THROW

1. Playing from behind

Identify one area where you feel *one of your children* or *your family as a whole* is "behind in the game." _____
_____
_____

Use the following questions to evaluate how you can encourage your child/family to "play from behind" to victory (use a separate piece of paper to write your answers):

- *Why* do you think your child/family is "behind in the game"? (By what standard of measurement?)
- How does your evaluation stack up against your family goals or expectations? (Check out your mission statement for the family or your children.)
- How might you redefine the terms of success (i.e., break the goal down into manageable steps so your child/family can "catch up one basket at a time")?
- How can you reinforce that your family team is "in the game together" so that everyone is supporting one another in reaching for the goal?
- Are you confident in your team's ability to win? How do you communicate that?
- In what way can you help your child/family focus on "how to win," not on the fact that they're "behind"?

2. Working yourself out of a job

For each of your children, list one thing that you're still doing for that child (or the family) that he or she should be doing for himself/herself (or the family). (Consider age, birth order, gender, physical or emotional maturity.) Depending on age, you might consider: number or type of household chores; home, yard, or car maintenance; managing personal finances or a portion of the family budget; purchase or care of clothes; shopping for or preparing family meals; transportation of child

and friends; etc. Then make a plan for giving each child more responsibility in that particular area.

- Child's name and age: _____
  Area in which I can give more responsibility: _____
  Plan for giving more responsibility: _____
  _____

- Child's name and age: _____
  Area in which I can give more responsibility: _____
  Plan for giving more responsibility: _____
  _____

- Child's name and age: _____
  Area in which I can give more responsibility: _____
  Plan for giving more responsibility: _____
  _____

- Child's name and age: _____
  Area in which I can give more responsibility: _____
  Plan for giving more responsibility: _____
  _____

3. Impacting future generations

If raising children is a spiritual activity, what kind of attention are
you giving to their spiritual foundation?

	Yes	No	Needs attention
I have a personal faith.			
My children know what I believe.			
I teach my children about God.			
I pray for my children.			
I pray with my spouse for our children.			
I pray with my children.			
We worship together as a family.			
We talk about how our faith applies to family activities and choices.			
Our family life is consistent with our spiritual values.			

AFTERWORD

"Write an afterword." This is what I was asked to do. To write a *word* . . . *after* the summer of 1999. A summer I will never forget.

Write a *word* . . . *after* one of the happiest days in Ricky's life. He had finally received the long-awaited news on *June 17* that Bethany House was going to publish his first book, *Coaching Your Kids in the Game of Life*. Now, not only was he a coach, he was an author! That made him feel really proud. He could have more players on his team than was ever possible before. Through this book he had the opportunity to impact millions of kids through coaching their parents. He felt that by equipping parents with effective parenting skills, he was helping kids in a tremendous way.

Write a *word* . . . *after* we celebrated his forty-third birthday on *June 24*. My little sister, Jocelyn, prepared a delicious soul food dinner, which we shared as a family with our dear friend Pastor Haman Cross Jr.

Write a *word* . . . *after* we celebrated with Dave and Neta on *June 25* at Old Orleans in downtown Evanston. Spicy chicken wings were one of Ricky's favorites. His stomach full of chicken wings did not compare with his heart full of gratitude to the Jacksons for their hard work and commitment to the book's success. He came bearing gifts as small tokens of his appreciation. We were all full of praise and thanks to God for His providence in bringing all of us together at The Worship Center and for His favor demonstrated toward us by providing a publisher.

Write a *word* . . . *after* Ricky was shot. One week later, on *July 2*, around 8:50 P.M. It was my mother's birthday, and a beautiful day in the neighborhood. He was just walking with his kids. Suddenly, shots were flying everywhere. One struck Ricky in the back.

Write a *word* . . . *after* his death at 12:42 A.M., *July 3*. I was in the critical care room alone with him. Whispering in his ear, "Live! Live! Come from the four winds, O breath of life, and breathe into this body slain."

Finally the nurse asked me, "You realize he's dead, don't you?" I looked at her in disbelief. Surely my ears had heard wrong. "He's dead?" I asked. "Yes." "He's dead?" I tried again. She answered an unchanging "Yes." "Dead?" "Yes."

The word that came to me after that was *"NO!"* And I just kept saying it over and over again, *"NO, NO, NO, NO, NO!"*

Now, almost four months later, I'm still trying to find the words to say after all these things. It's difficult. They escape me. They are not to be found inside my finite, human brain. Ricky's sudden death is still incomprehensible to me. When I had my first lengthy discussion with our children—Sabrina, twelve; Kelley, ten; and Ricky Jr., then eight—trying to explain their father's death, I could only turn to the words that are in the Holy Bible, for only it contains words that are eternally truth and life.

I read to them Ecclesiastes 3:1-2, "To everything there is a season, and a time for every matter under heaven. A time to be born, and a time to die." I explained that their daddy's time to be born was June 24, 1956, and his time to die was July 3, 1999. These times were set before the world was ever created. I explained that God has work for every person to do and that their father had finished his work here on earth and God had welcomed him into heaven. They look forward to seeing him again and spending time with him throughout eternity.

I believe that God is sovereign. He is in control of every situation and circumstance. I also believe that He is good and that He works all things together for good. Therefore, I thank Him and am forever grateful for the twenty-seven years that Ricky and I shared together and for the physical and spiritual fruit that our lives bore. He was God's gift to me and a blessing in my life. He will always hold a very precious and dear place in my heart. His legacy lives on in my life, in the lives of our three children, and in the lives of the thousands of people whom he touched. His life's work will continue through The Ricky Byrdsong Foundation.[1]

Many people have asked me, "What kind of a person was your husband?" He was special. He was one-of-a-kind.

One year after we met he was voted "Most Cooperative" by his high school senior classmates. This communicates Ricky's ability to touch other people's lives so that they felt connected to him and blessed by him. After spending only a short time with him, you felt as if you had grown up next door to him or had known him all your life (or wished that you had). Each encounter that he had with others was meaningful

---

[1]For more information, contact The Ricky Byrdsong Foundation, 2101 Dempster St., Evanston, IL 60201

and left an impact on them. He reached out to others and made them feel important. He looked for and amplified the good in everyone.

Ricky was a Simon Peter. A man of action. A doer. This trait, coupled with his cooperative and sensitive spirit, made him passionate about meeting other people's needs. He was a man with a plan, and whatever he worked on he worked on it with all his heart. His mind was constantly active, thinking about what he would do next, as soon as he finished what he was presently doing.

Ricky possessed tremendous self-discipline, willpower, and tenacity. Many times during his life he would go on extended fasts. He would spend as much time as he could studying the Bible and praying, seeking God's wisdom and direction on how he could serve humanity and advance God's kingdom here on earth.

He was always raising the standard, challenging others to try harder, do better, and achieve their maximum potential. He called people out of their drowsiness, laziness, and comfort zones, and challenged the status quo. In February 1997 he organized and led a national week of prayer and turning off the TV.

Yet at the same time he was fun to be with. He was the life of the party. He could tell stories (true ones!) and jokes that would keep you rolling for hours.

And . . . he had a smile. What a smile! It was infectious. It was contagious. It warmed your heart. It could win you over. It could make you change your mind. It attracted you to him. It let you know that you could trust him. It gave you a glimpse of the love and warmth that was inside his heart.

This is the kind of man Ricky Allen Byrdsong was.

I believe that a person is indestructible before his time. But July 3, 1999, was Ricky's appointed time to die. And he was ready. He had lived each day as if it were his last. That's why he had such an urgency about the things that he wanted to accomplish, such as finishing this book and writing a mission statement for our children.

Ricky "fought the good fight" and "kept the faith." He had "finished his course" (2 Timothy 4:7). He had reached a point of maturity, peace, and rest in his soul that all he wanted to do was God's will. Other things did not matter. That is what he so passionately expressed in his sermon when he kept saying, "It doesn't matter now." He could say like Paul in Philippians 1:20-21, "According to my earnest expectation and my hope, that in nothing I shall be ashamed, but that with all boldness, as always, so now also Christ shall be magnified in my body, whether it be by life, or by death. For to me to live is Christ, and to die is gain."

I would like to close by sharing Ricky's favorite quote. It was the one that most impacted and transformed his life, thinking, and teaching. He taught it diligently to our children. He lived by it daily. It says,

> The longer I live, the more I realize the impact of attitude on life. Attitude, to me, is more important than facts. It is more important than past, than education, than money, than circumstances, than failures, than successes, than what other people think or say or do. It is more important than appearance, giftedness or skill. It will make or break a company . . . a church . . . a home. The remarkable thing is we have a choice every day regarding the attitude we will embrace for that day. We cannot change our past...we cannot change the fact that people will act in a certain way. We cannot change the inevitable. The only thing we can do is play on the one string we have and that is our attitude. . . . I am convinced that life is 10 percent what happens to me and 90 percent how I react to it. And so it is with you . . . we are in charge of our attitudes.[2]

Ricky played on this one string well. *He was a one-string virtuoso.* In this, he receives my thunderous applause.

I believe that he would want to tell us right now, "You cannot change fact. You cannot change the past. But you can change the future. Play on your one string well. The game ain't over yet!" Ricky would want us to maintain an attitude of hope and confidence in our youth and an attitude of perseverance as we coach them in the game of life.

Ricky fulfilled God's purpose for his life, and in the same way we must fulfill ours. It was his desire for us. That's why he wrote this book.

My prayer is that you will put into practice the principles that have been presented within these pages. They will truly help your kids to win in the game of life.

Remember . . . they can't afford to lose.

—Sherialyn Byrdsong
October 26, 1999

---

[2]Charles R. Swindoll, *Strengthening Your Grip*, (Dallas: Word, Inc., 1982).

Mission Statement for the Byrdsong Children

Sabrina, Kelley, and Ricky are first of all grateful. They understand that to have breath each day is God's gift to them, but how they live their lives is their gift to God. They have been blessed with the Holy Spirit and bear the fruit of love, joy, peace, patience, kindness, goodness, faithfulness, gentleness, and self-control. "Please" and "Thank you" are two of their frequent expressions. They know that winners are "made" and not "born." They are confident that God has placed in them all the qualities they need to be winners. They understand that they must develop and use these qualities to their fullest potential. They give 100 percent effort in every endeavor. They are not afraid to try anything, because they know that to not try is the biggest failure of all. They are confident that they will enjoy success in every area of their lives and that they are richly blessed. They will share the fruit of their success with others, never forgetting that their achievements are God's gifts to them.

Kelley, Ricky, and Sabrina will not experiment with drugs, alcohol, cigarettes, or any other destructive substance. They will have the courage to say NO when offered any such vice. They will respectfully, yet boldly, reject any philosophy that is contrary to the Word of God. They know that they are responsible for their actions and will not seek to blame others for the choices they make.

They will treat all people, even their enemies, the way they would like to be treated. They will obey their parents and seek their guidance regarding the issues of life. They are assured that they will never lose the love of their parents. They understand that their parents' discipline is proof of their deep love for them.

Ricky, Sabrina, and Kelley may learn from many people along the path of life, but they will always look to the Holy Scriptures as their ultimate source of wisdom and knowledge. Jesus Christ is their perfect teacher and role model. People will remember these three because of their great compassion for others. When their lives are over, God will say to each one, "Well done, good and faithful servant!"

—Ricky Allen Byrdsong

A Northwestern Player's Mission Statement

A Northwestern basketball player is first of all grateful. He knows that only a fraction of one percent of young men playing basketball will have the privilege of competing at the college level. He accepts the fact that he is a role model, and that he is representing not only himself but the institution, his family, and his teammates. He sees his experience at Northwestern as a mechanism for making his mark on society. He is confident yet humble, never allowing his ego to emerge. He is proud of his strengths and keenly aware of his weaknesses, therefore, is always striving to improve upon his skills.

A Northwestern basketball player is always more concerned with the good of his team. He realizes that "no man is an island." Therefore, he appreciates the contributions of each team member, past and present. He understands that because much has been given to him, much will be demanded of him. He knows that the challenges of every practice and game will better prepare him for life. While he is relentless on both ends of the court, he knows that the other team is not his real opponent; it is the full extent of his own potential that he is always competing against.

A Northwestern basketball player understands that without discipline, true success cannot be achieved. He appreciates his coach's praise and he accepts his criticism, understanding that both are necessary for him to reach his fullest potential. He is courageous in the face of adversity, has unquestionable integrity, and infectious enthusiasm. He never allows excuses to stand in the way of his responsibilities. He is always focused, never involving himself with the decisions of the officials or the distractions of taunting fans.

A Northwestern basketball player is made and not born. Therefore, he understands that what he becomes is dependent upon his personal commitment to excellence. As he is always competing to win, he understands that winning will not be the true measure of his success; it will be how much of himself he has given to the game. In the end, his personal commitment to excellence combined with his God-given ability will make him an asset to the game and to the world around him.

—Coach Byrdsong, 1994

THE
RICKY BYRDSONG
FOUNDATION

■

The mission of
The Ricky Byrdsong Foundation
is to arrest the growing epidemic of
hate and violence in our society
by and against our youth.
By providing opportunities
that broaden perspective,
build character, and
instill a sense of purpose,
the foundation promotes reconciliation
and champions diversity.

2101 Dempster, Evanston, IL 60201
877-BRDSONG (877-273-7664)

BOLD HOPE
FOR YOUR FAMILY

Parenting the Wild Child
by Miles McPherson
Hope for Desperate Parents

Parenting the Wild Child provides the help you need when you don't know where to turn. Typical teen problems—chronic curfew breaking, defiant attitudes, drug use—still are common, but added to these are even more dangerous and alluring problems. Gangs, counterculture groups, and many more frightening behaviors are tearing teens right out of loving homes.

McPherson's suggestion is to look at misbehavior as a spiritual cancer. We all have the cellular capacity for cancer, but not everyone experiences the uncontrolled malignant growth. And just as there are many cancer treatments, so are there many ways to "*treat*" rebellious teens. Providing biblically based hope and direction for you and your teens, *Parenting the Wild Child* strives to bring effective healing and wholeness to your family.

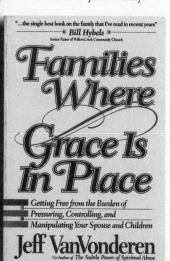

Families Where Grace is in Place
by Jeff VanVonderen
Transform Your Marriage and Parenting
You put your best efforts toward having a Christian marriage and raising Christian kids. But often you end up tired, discouraged, and feeling like a failure. This book shows how you can stop trying to "fix" your family members and leave that work to God.

Our responsibility is to serve our families and equip them to be their best. Healthy family relationships are only possible when the filter of God's grace is placed over the processes of marriage and parenting.

◈ BETHANYHOUSE
11400 Hampshire Avenue S. • Minneapolis, MN 55438
(800) 328-6109 • www.bethanyhouse.com